BIDWELL'S GUIDE
TO
GOVERNMENT MINISTERS

25.00

BIDWELL'S GUIDE
TO
GOVERNMENT
MINISTERS

VOLUME III

The British Empire and Successor States
1900–1972

Compiled and edited by

ROBIN BIDWELL

Secretary of the Middle East Centre, University of Cambridge

FRANK CASS : LONDON

First published 1974 in Great Britain by
FRANK CASS AND COMPANY LIMITED
67 Great Russell Street, London WC1B 3BT, England

and in United States of America by
FRANK CASS AND COMPANY LIMITED
c/o International Scholarly Book Services, Inc.
P.O. Box 4347, Portland, Oregon 97208

ISBN 0 7146 3017 9

Library of Congress Catalog Card No. 72–92958

Printed in Great Britain by
Unwin Brothers Limited
The Gresham Press, Old Woking, Surrey GU22 9LH
A member of the Staples Printing Group

To C.B.

How to use this book

I have divided this book into seven sections. It seemed appropriate to arrange this volume differently from the two previous ones. Europe and the Arab World are both geographical units in addition to having political ties, and I therefore grouped the Ministers together by office: the Prime Ministers of all the countries are followed by the Foreign Ministers of all the countries, and so on. The Commonwealth is so scattered that it seemed better to complete each section of countries before moving on to the next.

Group A consists of the "Old Commonwealth"—those countries which had governments before 1939. This comprises Great Britain, Canada, Australia, New Zealand, South Africa and (Southern) Rhodesia. I have listed Heads of State or Governors, Premiers, Ministers of Foreign Affairs, Defence, the Interior, and Finance. British Home Secretaries have been omitted as they were not particularly relevant in this connection. In their place I have put the Secretaries of State for the Colonies and Dominions and their successors.

Group B contains the countries of Asia. These are India, Pakistan, Burma, Ceylon, Malaya, Singapore, and Bangladesh. The first part gives the Viceroys, Secretaries of State for India and Burma, and the Governors of Burma, Ceylon and the Straits Settlements. After that, Heads of State follow in the normal sequence.

In Group C will be found the Mediterranean States—Gibraltar, Malta, Cyprus and Palestine/Israel.

Group D consists of the West and East African members of the Commonwealth—Nigeria, Gold Coast/Ghana, Gambia, Sierra Leone, Kenya, Uganda and Tanganyika/Tanzania.

Group E lists the States of Southern Africa—Mauritius, Nyasaland/Malawi, Northern Rhodesia/Zambia, and the former High Commission territories of Lesotho, Botswana and Swaziland.

Group F contains those Caribbean States which have either achieved independence or have an almost complete Cabinet system. These are Bahamas, Barbados, British Guiana/Guyana, British Honduras, Jamaica, and Trinidad and Tobago. As with all the previous Groups, the Ministers are listed in the normal sequence except that there are no Ministers of Defence. Where the post exists, it has always—except for a very short period in Jamaica—been held by the Prime Minister.

Group G is a mixture, for it contains all the States for which the standard list of five leading Ministers is not appropriate. Firstly there is the Pacific, for which the Rulers and Premiers of Tonga, the High Commissioners for the Western Pacific, the Governors and Premiers of Fiji, the President of Nauru, and the Rulers and Premiers of Western Samoa, are given. These are followed by the Premiers or Chief Ministers of the Canadian Provinces, the Australian States, the Indian States, the Leeward and Windward Islands, and the book concludes with Malayan Sultans.

Each Minister is listed with the date of his assumption of office, and each new page begins with the names of those whose appointments were the last to be announced for those offices. Each Minister should be assumed to have continued in power until a new name appears in his column. On a new page only the last name is given, and for his full name it will be necessary to turn back to the date of his appointment. An example will show how the book works. Let us assume that it is desired to find out who was the Canadian Minister of Foreign Affairs at the time of the Suez Crisis of November 1956. Canada is in Group A, and one turns to the Minister of Foreign Affairs in that section. The first appointment after November 1956 is that of John Diefenbaker on 21 June 1957. The name given above his is that of the Minister in power before him: Pearson. By turning back, one can see that his full name was Lester Bowles Pearson, and that he was appointed on 10 September 1948.

Contents

Introduction

This book is the third of a series designed to list the leading Ministers of the greater part of the world. The conception of grouping these countries together needs no apology: one reads of meetings of Commonwealth Heads of Government, of the Finance Ministers, and there are frequent exchanges of visits on a bilateral basis. The title *British Empire and Successor States* does, however, require explanation. In the past decade South Africa, Rhodesia and Pakistan have left the Commonwealth and it would be absurd to pretend that by this action these States ceased to exist. Their Ministers often continued in close contact with their former partners. I have also included two other States which occupy territory that once was red on the map, but which have never been part of the Commonwealth since achieving independence. Burma still has relations with its Commonwealth neighbours and it seemed useful, although extremely difficult, to list is Ministers. Israel, although I do not regard it as the legitimate successor of the whole of the Palestine Mandate, is part of the Mediterranean world—all of those other members are to be found either in Volume I or Volume II.

In order to avoid excessive bulk, I have restricted these tables to officials of primary importance. I have listed Heads of State or Governors, Premiers, Ministers of Foreign Affairs, Defence, the Interior and Finance. Where there has been an interregnum, I have not recorded the fact but merely listed the new incumbents on the day on which they took office. This is in no sense a history of the Commonwealth and I have restricted notes to a minimum. Thus, as a colony moved towards independence its political leader might become First Minister, then Chief Minister, then Premier, and finally Prime Minister. If details of this process are required they can easily be found in standard reference books. I have, however, noted the change of a Governor into a Governor-General or a Governor-General into a President because these are major steps towards independence. Any appointment after a State left the Commonwealth has been put in italics so as to make the position clearer. Thus, the name of Ian Smith does not appear in italics when he took office because Rhodesia was then still in the Commonwealth. References to him and his Ministers after the Unilateral Declaration of Independence, however, are italicised. When a Minister died in office I have not listed a short vacancy in a post. When a new Minister has been appointed *ad interim* I have indicated this with an asterisk if he did not subsequently keep the portfolio, but if he was later confirmed in office, I have merely put the first date.

It has not been possible to be entirely consistent in giving dates because weeks and even months sometimes elapsed between the announcement of an appointment and the actual assumption of office. In the days before air travel as much as six months may have passed between the nomination of a new Governor-General of Australia and his arrival in Canberra. As far as possible I have given the date of the taking of the oath of office. Similarly widely varying dates are given for Malayan rulers—in one case four years seem to have separated the succession of a Raja and his formal coronation. Either date may be given by the sources but I have always tried to give the earlier. Similarly, it has not been possible always to be consistent with the spelling of names—particularly for countries where other alphabets are used. In general I have tried to find the name in an official publication and to use that version of it.

While, naturally, all mistakes are my own, I should like to record my thanks for help on specific points to the offices of the High Commissioners for New Zealand, Malawi, Botswana, and Lesotho. Also the Ministry of Defence of Rhodesia kindly answered questions on dates for me. I am very grateful to the staff of the Official Publications Room of Cambridge University Library who staggered uncomplainingly under huge burdens of Gazettes and Year Books for me. These were the main sources of this book.

Cambridge
January 1973

ROBIN BIDWELL

		GREAT BRITAIN	CANADA	AUSTRALIA	NEW ZEALAND	SOUTH AFRICA	SOUTHERN RHODESIA
1900	1 Jan	Victoria	Earl of Minto		Earl of Ranfurly		
1901	1 Jan			Earl of Hopetoun			
	22 Jan	Edward VII					
1902	17 July			Lord Tennyson			
1904	21 Jan			Lord Northcote			
	20 June				Lord Plunket		
	10 Dec		Earl Grey				
1908	9 Sept			Earl of Dudley			
1910	6 May	George V					
	31 May					Lord Gladstone	
	22 June				Lord Islington		
1911	31 July			Lord Denman			
	13 Oct		Field-Marshal H. R. H. the Duke of Connaught				
1912	12 Dec				Earl of Liverpool *(Note 1)*		
1914	18 May			Sir Ronald Ferguson, Lord Novar			
	8 Sept					Lord Buxton	
1916	11 Nov		Duke of Devonshire				
1920	27 Sept				Admiral of the Fleet Earl Jellicoe		
	6 Oct			Lord Forster			
	Nov					Prince Arthur of Connaught	
1921	11 Aug		General Lord Byng				
1923	1 Oct						Colonel Sir John Chancellor
1924	21 Jan					Earl of Athlone	
	13 Dec				General Sir Charles Fergusson		

	GREAT BRITAIN	CANADA	AUSTRALIA	NEW ZEALAND	SOUTH AFRICA	SOUTHERN RHODESIA
	George V	Byng	Forster	Fergusson	Athlone	Chancellor
1925 8 Oct			Sir John Baird, Lord Stonehaven			
1926		Lord Willingdon				
1928 24 Nov						Sir Cecil Rodwell
1930 18 Mar				Lord Bledisloe		
1931 22 Jan			Sir Isaac Isaacs			
26 Jan					Earl of Clarendon	
4 Apr		Lord Bessborough				
1935 8 Jan						Sir Herbert James Stanley
12 Apr				Lord Galway		
4 Nov		John Buchan Lord Tweedsmuir				
1936 20 Jan	Edward VIII					
23 Jan			General Lord Gowrie V.C.			
11 Dec	George VI					
1937 5 Apr				Patrick Duncan		
1940 21 June		Earl of Athlone				
1941 22 Feb				Marshal of the R.A.F. Lord Newall		
1942 28 July						Sir Evelyn Baring
1943 17 July					Nicolaas Jacobus de Wet	
1944 20 Nov						Admiral Sir Charles Campbell Tait
1945 30 Jan			H.R.H. the Duke of Gloucester			
1946 1 Jan					Gideon Brand van Zyl	
12 Apr		Field-Marshal Earl Alexander				

		GREAT BRITAIN	CANADA	AUSTRALIA	NEW ZEALAND	SOUTH AFRICA	SOUTHERN RHODESIA
		George VI	Alexander	Gloucester	Newall	van Zyl	Tait
1946	17 June				General Lord Freyberg V. C.		
1947	25 Jan						General Sir John Noble Kennedy (Note 2)
	11 Mar			Sir William John McKell			
1951	1 Jan					Ernest George Jansen	
1952	6 Feb	Elizabeth II					
	28 Feb		Vincent Massey				
	2 Dec				General Lord Norrie		
1953	8 May			Field-Marshal Lord Slim			
1954	Nov						Admiral Sir Peveril William-Powlett
1957	5 Sept				Lord Cobham		
1959	15 Sept		General Georges Philias Vanier				
	23 Dec						Sir Humphrey Vicary Gibbs (Note 3)
1960	12 Jan					Charles Robberts Swart (Note 4)	
	2 Feb			Lord Dunrossil			
1961	3 Aug			Lord De Lisle V.C.			
1962	9 Nov				Brigadier Sir Bernard Fergusson		
1965	22 Sept			Lord Casey			
	18 Nov						*Clifford Walter Dupont (Note 5)*
1967	17 Apr		Roland Michener				

		GREAT BRITAIN	CANADA	AUSTRALIA	NEW ZEALAND	SOUTH AFRICA	RHODESIA
		Elizabeth II	Michener	Casey	Fergusson	Swart	Dupont
1967	1 June					*Jozua Francois Naudé (Note 6)*	
	1 Dec				Sir Arthur Porritt		
1968	10 Apr					*Jacobus Johannes Fouché*	
1969	30 Apr			Sir Paul Hasluck			
1972	27 Sept				Sir Denis Blundell		

		GREAT BRITAIN	CANADA	AUSTRALIA	NEW ZEALAND	SOUTH AFRICA	SOUTHERN RHODESIA
1900	1 Jan	Lord Salisbury	Sir Wilfrid Laurier		Richard John Seddon		
1901	1 Jan			Sir Edmund Barton			
1902	12 July	Arthur James Balfour					
1903	24 Sept			Alfred Deakin			
1904	27 Apr			John Christian Watson			
	18 Aug			George Houston Reid			
1905	5 July			Alfred Deakin			
	5 Dec	Sir Henry Campbell Bannerman					
1906	10 June				*William Hall-Jones		
	6 Aug				Sir Joseph George Ward		
1908	7 Apr	Herbert Henry Asquith					
	13 Nov			Andrew Fisher			
1909	2 June			Alfred Deakin			
1910	29 Apr			Andrew Fisher			
	31 May					General Louis Botha	
1911	10 Oct		Sir Robert Laird Borden				
1912	28 Mar				Thomas Mackenzie		
	10 July				William Ferguson Massey		
1913	24 June			Joseph Cook			
1914	17 Sept			Andrew Fisher			
1915	27 Oct			William Morris Hughes			
1916	7 Dec	David Lloyd George					

		GREAT BRITAIN	CANADA	AUSTRALIA	NEW ZEALAND	SOUTH AFRICA	SOUTHERN RHODESIA
		Lloyd George	Borden	Hughes	Massey	Botha	
1919	3 Sept					General Jan Christiaan Smuts	
1920	10 July		Arthur Meighen				
1921	29 Dec		Willaim Lyon Mackenzie King				
1922	23 Oct	Andrew Bonar Law					
1923	9 Feb			Stanley Melbourne Bruce			
	22 May	Stanley Baldwin					
	1 Oct						Sir Charles Coghlan
1924	22 Jan	James Ramsay MacDonald					
	30 June					General James Barry Munnik Hertzog	
	4 Nov	Stanley Baldwin					
1925	10 May				Sir Francis Bell		
	30 May				Joseph Gordon Coates		
1926	28 June		Arthur Meighen				
	25 Sept		William Lyon Mackenzie King				
1927	2 Sept						Howard Unwin Moffat
1928	10 Dec				Sir Joseph George Ward		
1929	5 June	James Ramsay MacDonald					
	22 Oct			James Henry Scullin			
1930	28 May				George William Forbes		

		GREAT BRITAIN	CANADA	AUSTRALIA	NEW ZEALAND	SOUTH AFRICA	SOUTHERN RHODESIA
		Macdonald	King	Scullin	Forbes	Hertzog	Moffatt
1930	7 Aug		Richard Bedford Bennett				
1932	6 Jan			Joseph Aloysius Lyons			
1933	6 July						George Mitchell
	12 Sept						Sir Godfrey Huggins later Lord Malvern
1935	7 June	Stanley Baldwin					
	23 Oct		William Lyon Mackenzie King				
	6 Dec				Michael Joseph Savage		
1937	28 May	Neville Chamberlain					
1939	7 Apr			Sir Earle Christmas Grafton Page			
	26 Apr			Robert Gordon Menzies			
	5 Sept					General Jan Christiaan Smuts	
1940	4 Apr				Peter Fraser		
	11 May	Winston Spencer Churchill					
1941	29 Aug			Arthur William Fadden			
	7 Oct			John Curtin			
1945	6 July			*Francis Michael Forde			
	13 July			Joseph Benedict Chifley			
	26 July	Clement Attlee					
1948	4 June					Dr Daniel Francois Malan	
	15 Nov		Louis Stephen St Laurent				

	GREAT BRITAIN	CANADA	AUSTRALIA	NEW ZEALAND	SOUTH AFRICA	SOUTHERN RHODESIA
	Attlee	St Laurent	Chifley	Fraser	Malan	Malvern
1949 13 Dec				Sidney George Holland		
19 Dec			Robert Gordon Menzies			
1951 26 Oct	Winston Spencer Churchill					
1953 7 Sept						Garfield Todd *(Note 7)*
1954 30 Nov					Johannes Gerhardus Strijdom	
1955 6 Apr	Anthony Eden					
1957 10 Jan	Harold Macmillan					
21 June		John Diefenbaker				
20 Sept				Keith Holyoake		
11 Dec				Sir Walter Nash		
1958 18 Feb						Sir Edgar Whitehead
2 Sept					Dr Hendrik Frensch Verwoerd	
1960 12 Dec				Sir Keith Holyoake		
1962 17 Dec						Winston Field
1963 22 Apr		Lester Pearson				
20 Oct	Sir Alec Douglas-Home					
1964 13 Apr						Ian Smith
16 Oct	Harold Wilson					
1966 26 Jan			Harold Edward Holt			
13 Sept					*Balthazar Johannes Vorster*	
1967 18 Dec			John McEwen			
1968 10 Jan			John Grey Gorton			
20 Apr		Pierre Elliott Trudeau				

		GREAT BRITAIN	CANADA	AUSTRALIA	NEW ZEALAND	SOUTH AFRICA	RHODESIA
		Wilson	Trudeau	Gorton	Holyoake	Vorster	Smith
1970	19 June	Edward Heath					
1971	10 Mar			William McMahon			
1972	7 Feb				John Marshall		
	5 Dec			Gough Whitlam			
	8 Dec				Norman Kirk		

		GREAT BRITAIN	CANADA	AUSTRALIA	NEW ZEALAND	SOUTH AFRICA	SOUTHERN RHODESIA
1900	1 Jan	Lord Salisbury	Richard William Scott *(Note 8)*				
	1 Nov	Lord Lansdowne					
1901	1 Jan			Sir Edmund Barton			
1903	24 Sept			Alfred Deakin			
1904	27 Apr			William Morris Hughes			
	18 Aug			George Houston Reid			
1905	5 July			Alfred Deakin			
	11 Dec	Sir Edward Grey					
1908	9 Oct		Charles Murphy				
	13 Nov			Egerton Lee Batchelor			
1909	2 June			Littleton Ernest Groom			
1910	29 Apr			Egerton Lee Batchelor			
1911	9 Oct		William James Roche				
	14 Oct			Josiah Thomas			
1912	29 Oct		Louis Coderre				
1913	24 June			Patrick McMahon Glynn			
1914	17 Sept			John Andrew Arthur			
	9 Dec			Hugh Mahon			
1915	6 Oct		Pierre Blondin				
1916	14 Nov			*None*			
	11 Dec	Arthur James Balfour					
1917	8 Jan		Esioff Léon Patenaude				
	12 Jun		*None*				
	12 Oct		Martin Burrell				

	GREAT BRITAIN	CANADA	AUSTRALIA	NEW ZEALAND	SOUTH AFRICA	SOUTHERN RHODESIA
	Balfour	Burrell				
1919 24 Oct	Lord Curzon					
27 Nov				Sir James Allen		
31 Dec		Arthur Lewis Sifton				
1920 17 May				Ernest Page Lee		
10 July		Arthur Meighen				
1921 21 Dec			William Morris Hughes			
29 Dec		William Lyon Mackenzie King				
1923 9 Feb			Stanley Melbourne Bruce			
26 June				Sir Francis Bell		
1924 23 Jan	James Ramsay MacDonald					
7 Nov	Sir Austen Chamberlain					
1926 23 May				William Nosworthy		
28 June		Arthur Meighen				
25 Sept		William Lyon Mackenzie King				
1927 1 June					General James Barry Munnik Hertzog	
1928 10 Dec				Sir Joseph George Ward		
1929 8 June	Arthur Henderson					
22 Oct			James Henry Scullin			
1930 28 May				George William Forbes		
7 Aug		Richard Bedford Bennett				
1931 26 Aug	Lord Reading					

		GREAT BRITAIN	CANADA	AUSTRALIA	NEW ZEALAND	SOUTH AFRICA	SOUTHERN RHODESIA
		Reading	Bennett	Scullin	Forbes	Hertzog	
1931	9 Nov	Sir John Simon					
1932	6 Jan			John Greig Latham			
1934	12 Oct			Sir George Foster Pearce			
1935	7 June	Sir Samuel Hoare					
	23 Oct		William Lyon Mackenzie King				
	6 Dec				Michael Joseph Savage		
	23 Dec	Anthony Eden					
1937	29 Nov			William Morris Hughes			
1938	22 Feb	Lord Halifax					
1939	26 Apr			Sir Henry Somer Gullett			
	6 Sept					General Jan Christiaan Smuts	
1940	14 Mar			John McEwen			
	30 Apr				Frank Langstone		
	28 Oct			Sir Frederick Harold Stewart			
	23 Dec	Anthony Eden					
1941	7 Oct			Herbert Vere Evatt			
1942	21 Dec				*Vacant*		
1943	7 July				Peter Fraser		
1945	26 July	Ernest Bevin					
1946	5 Sept		Louis St Laurent				
1948	4 June					Dr Daniel Francois Malan	
	10 Sept		Lester Bowles Pearson				

	GREAT BRITAIN	CANADA	AUSTRALIA	NEW ZEALAND	SOUTH AFRICA	SOUTHERN RHODESIA
	Bevin	Pearson	Evatt	Fraser	Malan	
1949 13 Dec				Frederick Widdowson Doidge		
19 Dec			Percy Claude Spender			
1951 9 Mar	Herbert Morrison					
26 Apr			Richard Gardiner Casey			
Sept				Thomas Clifton Webb		
27 Oct	Anthony Eden					
1953 1 Aug						*(Note 9)*
1954 26 Nov				Thomas Lachlan Macdonald		
30 Nov					Eric Louw	
1955 6 Apr	Harold Macmillan					
20 Dec	Selwyn Lloyd					
1957 21 June		John Diefenbaker				
12 Sept		Sidney Earle Smith				
11 Dec				Sir Walter Nash		
1959 18 Mar		John Diefenbaker				
4 June		Howard Charles Green				
1960 4 Feb			Robert Gordon Menzies			
27 July	Lord Home					
12 Dec				Sir Keith Holyoake		
1961 22 Dec			Sir Garfield Edward John Barwick			
1963 22 Apr		Paul Joseph Martin				
20 Oct	Richard Austen Butler					
1964 9 Jan					*Dr Hilgard Muller*	

		GREAT BRITAIN	CANADA	AUSTRALIA	NEW ZEALAND	SOUTH AFRICA	SOUTHERN RHODESIA
		Butler	Martin	Barwick	Holyoake	Muller	
1964	14 Apr						Ian Douglas Smith
	24 Apr			Paul Meerna Caedwalla Hasluck			
	19 Aug						Clifford Walter Dupont
	16 Oct	Patrick Gordon Walker					
1965	22 Jan	Michael Stewart					
	31 Dec						*Lord Graham*
1966	10 Aug	George Brown					
1968	15 Mar	Michael Stewart					
	20 Apr		Mitchell Sharp				
	13 Sept						*John Howman*
1969	10 Feb			Gordon Freeth			
	11 Nov			William McMahon			
1970	19 June	Sir Alec Douglas-Home					
1971	21 Mar			Leslie Bury			
	1 Aug			Nigel Bowen			
1972	5 Dec			Gough Whitlam			
	8 Dec				Norman Kirk		

	GREAT BRITAIN	CANADA	AUSTRALIA	NEW ZEALAND	SOUTH AFRICA	SOUTHERN RHODESIA
1900 1 Jan	Lord Lansdowne	Sir Frederick William Borden		Richard John Seddon		
1 Nov	William St John Brodrick					
1901 1 Jan			Sir James Robert Dickson			
10 Jan			Sir John Forrest			
1903 7 Aug			James George Drake			
24 Sept			Austin Chapman			
12 Oct	Hugh Arnold-Forster					
1904 27 Apr			Anderson Dawson			
18 Aug			James Whiteside McCay			
1905 5 July			Thomas Playford			
11 Dec	Richard Burdon Haldane					
1906 10 June				Albert Pitt		
18 Nov				Sir Joseph George Ward		
1907 24 Jan			Thomas Thomson Ewing			
1908 13 Nov			George Foster Pearce			
1909 2 June			Joseph Cook			
1910 29 Apr			George Foster Pearce			
31 May					General Jan Christiaan Smuts	
1911 10 Oct		General Sir Sam Hughes				
1912 28 Mar				*None Announced*		
14 June	John Edward Bernard Seely					
10 July				Sir James Allen		

	GREAT BRITAIN	CANADA	AUSTRALIA	NEW ZEALAND	SOUTH AFRICA	SOUTHERN RHODESIA
	Seely	Hughes	Pearce	Allen	Smuts	
1913 24 June			Edward Davis Millen			
1914 31 Mar	Herbert Henry Asquith					
6 Aug	Field-Marshal Earl Kitchener of Khartoum					
17 Sept			George Foster Pearce			
1916 7 July	David Lloyd George					
23 Nov		Sir Albert Edward Kemp *(Note 10)*				
11 Dec	Lord Derby					
1917 12 Oct		General Sydney Mewburn				
1918 20 Apr	Lord Milner					
1919 14 Jan	Winston Spencer Churchill					
1920 24 Jan		Hugh Guthrie				
19 Mar					Colonel Hendrik Mentz	
17 May				*Joseph Gordon Coates		
5 Aug				Sir Robert Heaton Rhodes		
1921 11 Feb	Sir Laming Worthington-Evans					
21 Dec			Walter Massy-Green			
29 Dec		George Perry Graham				
1922 25 Oct	Lord Derby					
1923 9 Feb			Eric Kendall Bowden			
28 Apr		Edward Mortimer Macdonald				

	GREAT BRITAIN	CANADA	AUSTRALIA	NEW ZEALAND	SOUTH AFRICA	SOUTHERN RHODESIA
	Derby	Macdonald	Bowden	Rhodes	Mentz	
1923 1 Oct						Major Robert Hudson
1924 23 Jan	Stephen Walsh					
30 June					Colonel Frederick Hugh Page Cresswell	
7 Nov	Sir Laming Worthington-Evans					
1925 16 Jan			Sir Neville Reginald Howse V.C.			
1926 23 May				Francis Joseph Rolleston		
13 July		Hugh Guthrie				
7 Oct		Colonel James Layton Ralston				
1927 2 Apr			Sir Thomas William Glasgow			
1928 10 Dec				Thomas Mason Wilford		
1929 8 June	Thomas Shaw					
22 Oct			Albert Ernest Green			
15 Dec				John George Cobbe		
1930 25 Aug		Colonel Donald Mathieson Sutherland				
1931 4 Feb			John Joseph Daly			
3 Mar			Joseph Benedict Chifley			
30 Aug	Lord Crewe					
9 Nov	Lord Hailsham					
1932 6 Jan			Sir George Foster Pearce			
1933 30 Mar					Oswald Pirow	

	GREAT BRITAIN	CANADA	AUSTRALIA	NEW ZEALAND	SOUTH AFRICA	SOUTHERN RHODESIA
	Hailsham	Sutherland	Pearce	Cobbe	Pirow	Hudson
1933 12 Sept						Stephen Martin Lanigan O'Keefe
1934 12 Oct			Sir Robert Archdale Parkhill			
14 Nov						Vernon Arthur Lewis
17 Nov		Grote Stirling				
1935 6 June	Lord Halifax					
23 Oct		Ian Mackenzie				
27 Nov	Alfred Duff Cooper					
6 Dec				Frederick Jones		
1936 12 Aug						Robert Clarkson Tredgold
1937 28 May	Leslie Hore-Belisha					
20 Nov			Joseph Aloysius Lyons			
29 Nov			Harold Victor Campbell Thorby			
1938 7 Nov			Brigadier Geoffrey Austin Street *(Note 11)*			
1939 6 Sept					General Jan Christiaan Smuts	
20 Sept		Norman McLeod Rogers				
1940 5 Jan	Oliver Stanley					
11 May	Anthony Eden					
13 June		James Layton Ralston				
14 Aug			*Philip Albert Martin McBride			
28 Oct			Percy Claude Spender			

	GREAT BRITAIN	CANADA	AUSTRALIA	NEW ZEALAND	SOUTH AFRICA	SOUTHERN RHODESIA
	Eden	Ralston	Spender	Jones	Smuts	Tredgold
1940 23 Dec	David Margesson					
1941 7 Oct			Francis Michael Forde (Note 12)			
1942 22 Feb	Sir James Grigg					
1943 1 Mar						Sir Godfrey Huggins
1944 2 Feb						Captain Frank Harris
2 Nov		General Andrew McNaughten				
1945 1 July						Colonel William Ralston
13 July			John Albert Beasley			
26 July	John James Lawson					
21 Aug		Douglas Charles Abbott				
1946 7 June						Colonel Sir Ernest Lucas Guest
15 Aug			Francis Michael Forde			
7 Oct	Frederick Bellenger					
1 Nov			John Johnstone Dedman			
12 Dec		Brooke Claxton				
1947 1 Jan	Albert Victor Alexander (Note 13)					
1948 4 June					Francois Christiaan Erasmus	
19 Nov						Sir Godfrey Huggins
1949 13 Dec				Thomas Lachlan Macdonald		
19 Dec			Eric John Harrison			

	GREAT BRITAIN	CANADA	AUSTRALIA	NEW ZEALAND	SOUTH AFRICA	SOUTHERN RHODESIA
	Alexander	Claxton	Harrison	Macdonald	Erasmus	Huggins
1950 28 Feb	Emmanuel Shinwell					
24 Oct			Sir Philip Albert Martin McBride			
1951 26 Oct	Winston Spencer Churchill					
1952 1 Mar	Field-Marshal Earl Alexander of Tunis					
1953 7 Sept						George Davenport *(Note 14)*
1954 1 Jul		Ralph Osborne Campney				
18 Oct	Harold Macmillan					
1955 6 Apr	Selwyn Lloyd					
20 Dec	Walter Monckton					
1956 18 Oct	Anthony Head					
1957 13 Jan	Duncan Sandys					
21 June		General George Randolph Pearkes V.C.				
20 Sept				Dean Eyre		
11 Dec				Philip George Connolly		
1958 10 Dec			Athol Gordon Townley			
1959 14 Oct	Harold Watkinson					
6 Dec					Jacobus Johannes Fouché	
1960 11 Oct		Douglas Scott Harkness				
12 Dec				Dean Eyre		
1962 16 July	Peter Thorneycroft					
1963 11 Feb		Gordon Minto Churchill				
22 Apr		Paul Theodore Hellyer				

	GREAT BRITAIN	CANADA	AUSTRALIA	NEW ZEALAND	SOUTH AFRICA	SOUTHERN RHODESIA
	Thorneycroft	Hellyer	Townley	Eyre	Fouché	Davenport
1963 18 Dec			Paul Meerna Caedwalla Hasluck			
1964 14 Apr						Ian Douglas Smith
24 Apr			Shane Dunne Paltridge			
14 Oct	Denis Healey					
1965 31 Dec						*Lord Graham*
1966 26 Jan			Allen Fairhall			
4 Apr					*Pieter Willem Botha*	
12 Dec				Brigadier David Thomson		
1967 18 Sept		Léo Alphonse Joseph Cadieux				
1968 11 Sept						*John Howman*
1969 11 Nov			John Malcolm Fraser			
1970 19 June	Lord Carrington					
24 Sept		Donald Macdonald				
1971 11 Mar			John Grey Gorton			
13 Aug			David Fairbairn			
1972 28 Jan		Edgar John Benson				
9 Feb				Allan McCready		
27 Nov		James Richardson				
5 Dec			Lance Barnard			
8 Dec				Arthur Faulkner		

BRITISH COLONIAL/DOMINION MINISTERS
MINISTERS OF THE INTERIOR

	GREAT BRITAIN COLONIAL SECRETARY	GREAT BRITAIN DOMINIONS SECRETARY	CANADA	AUSTRALIA	NEW ZEALAND	SOUTH AFRICA	SOUTHERN RHODESIA
1900 1 Jan	Joseph Chamberlain		Clifford Sifton				
1901 1 Jan				Sir William John Lyne			
1903 7 Aug				Sir John Forrest			
9 Oct	Alfred Lyttleton						
1904 27 Apr				Egerton Lee Batchelor			
18 Aug				Dugald Thomson			
1905 8 Apr			Frank Oliver				
5 July				Littleton Ernest Groom			
11 Dec	Lord Elgin						
1906 12 Oct				Thomas Thomson Ewing			
1907 24 Jan				John Henry Keating			
1908 16 Apr	Lord Crewe						
13 Nov				Hugh Mahon			
1909 9 Jan					David Buddo		
2 June				George Warburton Fuller			
1910 29 Apr				King O'Malley			
31 May						General Jan Christiaan Smuts	
7 Nov	Lewis Harcourt						
1911 10 Oct			Robert Rogers				
1912 19 March					George Warren Russell		
26 June						Abraham Fischer	
10 July					Francis Bell		
29 Oct			William James Roche				

	GREAT BRITAIN COLONIAL SECRETARY	GREAT BRITAIN DOMINIONS SECRETARY	CANADA	AUSTRALIA	NEW ZEALAND	SOUTH AFRICA	SOUTHERN RHODESIA
	Harcourt		Roche	O'Malley	Bell	Fischer	
1913 24 June				Joseph Cook			
16 Nov						*Vacant*	
1914 17 Sept				William Oliver Archibald			
1915 27 May	Andrew Bonar Law						
6 Aug					George Warren Russell		
27 Oct				King O'Malley			
1916 1 Feb						Sir Thomas Watt	
14 Nov				Frederick William Bamford			
11 Dec	Walter Long						
1917 17 Feb				Patrick McMahon Glynn			
12 Oct			Arthur Meighen				
1919 9 Jan	Lord Milner						
5 Sept					John Bird Hine		
1920 4 Feb				Alexander Poynton			
20 June					George James Anderson		
10 July			Sir James Alexander Lougheed				
1921 14 Feb	Winston Spencer Churchill						
1 Mar					William Downie Stewart		
10 Mar						Patrick Duncan	
21 Dec				George Foster Pearce			
29 Dec			Charles Stewart				
1922 25 Oct	Duke of Devonshire						

	GREAT BRITAIN COLONIAL SECRETARY	GREAT BRITAIN DOMINIONS SECRETARY	CANADA	AUSTRALIA	NEW ZEALAND	SOUTH AFRICA	SOUTHERN RHODESIA
	Devonshire		Stewart	Pearce	Stewart	Duncan	
1923 26 June					Richard Francis Bollard		
1924 23 Jan	James Henry Thomas						
30 June						Dr Daniel Francois Malan	
7 Nov	Leopold Amery	Leopold Amery					
1926 18 June				Sir Thomas Glasgow			
13 July			Richard Bedford Bennett				
25 Sept			Charles Stewart				
1927 2 Apr				Charles William Clanan Marr			
Sept					*Sir Maui Pomare		
1928 24 Feb				Sir Neville Reginald Howse V.C.			
29 Nov				Charles Lydiard Aubrey Abbott			
10 Dec					Philip Aldborough de la Perrelle		
1929 8 June	Sydney Webb Lord Passfield	Sydney Webb Lord Passfield					
22 Oct				Arthur Blakeley			
1930 13 June		James Henry Thomas					
7 Aug			Thomas Gerow Murphy				
1931 26 Aug	James Henry Thomas						
22 Sept					Adam Hamilton		
9 Nov	Sir Philip Cunliffe-Lister Lord Swinton						

	GREAT BRITAIN COLONIAL SECRETARY	GREAT BRITAIN DOMINIONS SECRETARY	CANADA	AUSTRALIA	NEW ZEALAND	SOUTH AFRICA	SOUTHERN RHODESIA
	Swinton	Thomas	Murphy	Blakeley	Hamilton	Malan	
1932 6 Jan				Sir Robert Archdale Parkhill			
13 Oct				John Arthur Perkins			
1933 20 Jan					James Alexander Young		
30 Mar						Jan Hendrik Hofmeyer	
5 July							William Muter Leggate *(Note 15)*
12 Sept							Stephen Martin Lanigan O'Keefe
1934 12 Oct				Eric John Harrison			
9 Nov				Thomas Paterson			
14 Nov							Vernon Arthur Lewis
1935 7 June	Malcolm MacDonald						
23 Oct			Thomas Crerar *(Note 16)*				
27 Nov	James Henry Thomas	Malcolm MacDonald					
1935 6 Dec					William Edward Parry		
1936 29 May	William Ormsby Gore Lord Harlech						
Sept							Sir Percy Fynn
28 Nov						Richard Stuttaford	
1937 29 Nov				John McEwen			
1938 16 May	Malcolm MacDonald	Lord Stanley					
4 Nov		Malcolm MacDonald					
1939 2 Feb		Sir Thomas Inskip Lord Caldecote					

	GREAT BRITAIN COLONIAL SECRETARY	GREAT BRITAIN DOMINIONS SECRETARY	CANADA	AUSTRALIA	NEW ZEALAND	SOUTH AFRICA	SOUTHERN RHODESIA
	MacDonald	Caldecote		McEwen	Parry	Stuttaford	Fynn
1939 26 Apr				Hattil Spencer Foll			
4 Sept		Anthony Eden					
6 Sept						Harry Gordon Lawrence	
3 Oct							Harry Davies
1940 15 May	Lord Lloyd	Lord Caldecote					
4 Oct		Lord Cranborne					
1941 8 Feb	Lord Moyne						
7 Oct					Joseph Silver Collings		
1942 18 Feb	Lord Cranborne	Clement Attlee					
22 Nov	Oliver Stanley						
1943 7 July						Charles Francis Clarkson	
24 Sept		Lord Cranborne					
12 Oct							*Sir Godfrey Huggins
1944 2 Feb							Colonel Sir Ernest Lucas Guest
1945 13 July					Herbert Victor Johnson		
26 July	George Henry Hall	Lord Addison *(Note 17)*					
1946 3 May							Hugh Beadle
1947 7 Oct	Arthur Creech Jones	Philip Noel-Baker					
1948 15 Jan						Harry Gordon Lawrence	
4 June						Dr Theophilus Ebenaeser Dönges	
1949 13 Dec					Sir William Bodkin		

	GREAT BRITAIN COLONIAL SECRETARY	GREAT BRITAIN DOMINIONS SECRETARY	CANADA	AUSTRALIA	NEW ZEALAND	SOUTH AFRICA	SOUTHERN RHODESIA
	Jones	Baker		Johnson	Bodkin	Dönges	Beadle
1949 19 Dec				Philip Albert Martin McBride			
1950 28 Feb	James Griffiths	Patrick Gordon Walker					
20 July							Julian MacDonald Greenfield
24 Oct				Eric John Harrison			
1951 11 May				Wilfrid Selwyn Kent Hughes			
26 Oct	Oliver Lyttleton	General Lord Ismay					
1952 12 Mar		Lord Salisbury					
24 Nov		Lord Swinton					
1954 28 Jan							Garfield Todd *(Note 18)*
28 July	Alan Lennox-Boyd						
17 Nov							Albert Rubidge Washington Stumbles
26 Nov					Sidney Walter Smith		
1955 12 Apr		Lord Home					
1956 11 Jan				Allen Fairhall			
1957 11 Dec					William Theophilus Anderton		
1958 14 Jan							Alan Davidson Hutchinson Lloyd
18 Feb							Reginald Knight
20 Oct						Jozua Francois Naudé	
10 Dec				Gordon Freeth			
1959 14 Oct	Iain Macleod						

	GREAT BRITAIN COLONIAL SECRETARY	GREAT BRITAIN DOMINIONS SECRETARY	CANADA	AUSTRALIA	NEW ZEALAND	SOUTH AFRICA	SOUTHERN RHODESIA
	Macleod	Home		Freeth	Anderton	Naudé	Knight
1960 27 July		Duncan Sandys					
12 Dec					Sir Frank Leon Gotz		
1961 2 Aug						*Johannes de Klerk*	
9 Oct	Reginald Maudling						
1962 16 July	Duncan Sandys						
23 Sept							Albert Rubidge Washington Stumbles
17 Dec							John Howman
1963 18 Dec				John Grey Gorton			
20 Dec					David Coutts Seath		
1964 4 Mar				John Douglas Anthony			
14 Apr							William John Harper
16 Oct	Anthony Greenwood	Arthur Bottomley					
1965 22 Dec	Lord Longford						
1966 4 Apr						*Pieter Matheus Kruger Le Roux*	
5 Apr	Fred Lee						
31 July	*Abolished*						
10 Aug		Herbert Bowden					
1967 28 Aug		George Thomson					
16 Oct				Peter Nixon			
1968 9 Aug						*Stefanus Louwrens Muller*	
16 Aug							Lance Smith
17 Oct		*Merged with Foreign Office*					
1970 12 May						*Marais Viljoen*	

	CANADA	AUSTRALIA	NEW ZEALAND	SOUTH AFRICA	RHODESIA
		Nixon	Seath	Viljoen	Smith
1970 19 Nov				*Theo Gerdener*	
1971 3 Feb		Ralph James Hunt			
1972 9 Feb			Alan Highet		
1 Aug				*Dr Connie Mulder*	
5 Dec		*None announced*			
8 Dec			Henry May		

	GREAT BRITAIN	CANADA	AUSTRALIA	NEW ZEALAND	SOUTH AFRICA	SOUTHERN RHODESIA
1900 1 Jan	Sir Michael Hicks-Beach	William Stevens Fielding		Richard John Seddon		
1901 1 Jan			Sir George Turner			
1902 12 July	Charles Ritchie					
1903 9 Oct	Austen Chamberlain					
1904 27 Apr			John Christian Watson			
18 Aug			Sir George Turner			
1905 5 July			Sir John Forrest			
11 Dec	Herbert Henry Asquith					
1906 10 June				William Hall-Jones		
6 Aug				Sir Joseph George Ward		
1907 30 July			Sir William John Lyne			
1908 16 Apr	David Lloyd George					
13 Nov			Andrew Fisher			
1909 2 June			Sir John Forrest			
1910 29 Apr			Andrew Fisher			
31 May					Henry Charles Hull	
1911 10 Oct		Sir William Thomas White				
1912 28 Mar				Arthur Mielziner Myers		
26 June					General Jan Christiaan Smuts	
10 July				James Allen		
1913 24 June			Sir John Forrest			
1914 17 Sept			Andrew Fisher			
1915 24 Feb					Sir David de Villiers Graaf	

	GREAT BRITAIN	CANADA	AUSTRALIA	NEW ZEALAND	SOUTH AFRICA	SOUTHERN RHODESIA
	Lloyd George	White	Fisher	Allen	Graaf	
1915 27 May	Reginald McKenna					
12 Aug				Sir Joseph George Ward		
27 Oct			William Guy Higgs			
1916 1 Feb					Henry Burton	
14 Nov			Alexander Poynton			
11 Dec	Andrew Bonar Law					
1917 17 Feb			Sir John Forrest			
4 Oct					Thomas Orr	
1918 27 Mar			William Alexander Watt			
1919 14 Jan	Austen Chamberlain					
2 Aug		Sir Henry Lumley Drayton				
1 Sept				Sir James Allen		
1920 19 Mar					Henry Burton	
17 May				William Ferguson Massey		
28 July			Sir Joseph Cook			
1921 5 Apr	Sir Robert Stevenson Horne					
21 Dec			Stanley Melbourne Bruce			
29 Dec		William Stevens Fielding				
1922 25 Oct	Stanley Baldwin					
1923 9 Feb			Earle Christmas Grafton Page			
1 Oct						Percy Fynn
11 Oct	Neville Chamberlain					
1924 23 Jan	Philip Snowden					

	GREAT BRITAIN	CANADA	AUSTRALIA	NEW ZEALAND	SOUTH AFRICA	SOUTHERN RHODESIA
	Snowden	Fielding	Page	Massey	Burton	Fynn
1924 30 June					Nicolaas Christiaan Havenga	
7 Nov	Winston Spencer Churchill					
1925 14 May				William Nosworthy		
5 Sept		James Alexander Robb				
1926 23 May				William Downie Stewart		
13 July		Richard Bedford Bennett				
25 Sept		James Alexander Robb				
1928 10 Dec				Sir Joseph George Ward		
1929 8 June	Philip Snowden					
22 Oct			Edward Granville Theodore			
26 Nov		Charles Avery Dunning				
1930 28 May				George William Forbes		
9 July			James Henry Scullin			
7 Aug		Richard Bedford Bennett				
1931 29 Jan			Edward Granville Theodore			
22 Sept				William Downie Stewart		
9 Nov	Neville Chamberlain					
1932 6 Jan			Joseph Aloysius Lyons			
3 Feb		Edgar Nelson Rhodes				
1933 20 Jan				Joseph Gordon Coates		

	GREAT BRITAIN	CANADA	AUSTRALIA	NEW ZEALAND	SOUTH AFRICA	SOUTHERN RHODESIA
	Chamberlain	Rhodes	Lyons	Coates	Havenga	Fynn
1933 12 Sept						Jacob Hendrik Smit
1935 3 Oct			Richard Gardiner Casey			
23 Oct		Charles Avery Dunning				
6 Dec				Walter Nash *(Note 19)*		
1937 28 May	Sir John Simon					
1939 26 Apr			Robert Gordon Menzies			
6 Sept		James Layton Ralston			Jan Hendrik Hofmeyer	
1940 14 Mar			Percy Claude Spender			
11 May	Sir Kingsley Wood					
8 July		James Lorimer Ilsley				
28 Oct			Arthur William Fadden			
1941 7 Oct			Joseph Benedict Chifley			
1942 26 Feb						Max Danziger
1943 24 Sept	Sir John Anderson					
1945 26 July	Hugh Dalton					
1946 3 May						Colonel Sir Ernest Lucas Guest
23 Sept						Edgar Whitehead
10 Dec		Douglas Charles Abbott				
1947 13 Nov	Sir Stafford Cripps					
1948 15 Jan					Frederick Sturrock	
4 June					Nicolaas Christiaan Havenga	

	GREAT BRITAIN	CANADA	AUSTRALIA	NEW ZEALAND	SOUTH AFRICA	SOUTHERN RHODESIA
	Cripps	Abbott	Chifley	Nash	Havenga	Whitehead
1949 13 Dec				Sidney George Holland		
19 Dec			Sir Arthur William Fadden			
1950 19 Oct	Hugh Gaitskell					
1951 26 Oct	Richard Austen Butler					
1953 7 Sept						Donald MacIntyre *(Note 20)*
1954 28 Jan						Cyril Hatty
1 July		Walter Edward Harris				
20 Nov				Jack Thomas Watts		
30 Nov					Eric Louw	
1955 20 Dec	Harold Macmillan					
1956 31 July					Jozua Francois Naudé	
1957 13 Jan	Peter Thorneycroft					
27 June		Donald Methuen Fleming				
11 Dec				Arnold Henry Nordmeyer		
1958 6 Jan	Derick Heathcoat Amory					
14 Jan						Abraham Eliezer Abrahamson
18 Feb						Cyril Hatty
20 Oct					Dr Theophilus Ebenaeser Dönges	
10 Dec			Harold Edward Holt			
1960 27 July	Selwyn Lloyd					
12 Dec				Harry Lake		
1962 16 July	Reginald Maudling					

	GREAT BRITAIN	CANADA	AUSTRALIA	NEW ZEALAND	SOUTH AFRICA	SOUTHERN RHODESIA
	Maudling	Fleming	Holt	Lake	Dönges	Hatty
1962 9 Aug		George Clyde Nowlan				
23 Sept						Geoffrey Ellman-Brown
17 Dec						Ian Douglas Smith
1963 22 Apr		Walter Lockhart Gordon				
1964 14 Apr						John James Wrathall
16 Oct	James Callaghan					
1965 18 Dec		Mitchell Sharp				
1966 26 Jan			William McMahon			
1967 24 Jan					*Dr Nicolaas Diederichs*	
3 Mar				Robert David Muldoon		
29 Nov	Roy Jenkins					
1968 22 Apr		Edgar John Benson				
1969 11 Nov			Leslie Bury			
1970 19 June	Iain Macleod					
25 July	Anthony Barber					
1971 21 Mar			Billy Mackie Snedden			
1972 28 Jan		John Napier Turner				
5 Dec			Gough Whitlam			
18 Dec				William Rowling		
19 Dec			Frank Crean			

		VICEROY	SECRETARY OF STATE	BURMA	CEYLON	STRAITS SETTLEMENTS
1900	1 Jan	Lord Curzon *(Note 21)*	Lord George Hamilton		Sir J. West Ridgeway	Colonel Sir Charles Mitchell
1901	5 Nov					Sir Frank Athelstane Swettenham
1903	9 Oct		William St John Brodrick			
	3 Dec				Sir Henry Blake	
1904	16 Apr					Sir John Anderson
1905	18 Nov	Earl of Minto				
	11 Dec		Lord Morley			
1907	24 Aug				Sir Henry McCallum	
1910	7 Nov		Lord Crewe			
	23 Nov	Lord Hardinge of Penshurst				
1911	2 Sept					Sir Arthur Henderson Young
1913	18 Oct				Sir Robert Chalmers	
1915	27 May		Austen Chamberlain			
1916	4 Apr	Lord Chelmsford				
	15 Apr				Sir John Anderson	
1917	20 July		Edwin Montagu			
1918	11 Sept				Brigadier-General Sir William Manning	
1920	7 Feb					Sir Laurence Guillemard
1921	2 Apr	Lord Reading				
1922	21 Mar		Lord Peel			
1923	1 Jan			Sir Harcourt Butler		
1924	23 Jan		Lord Olivier			
	7 Nov		Lord Birkenhead			
1925	30 Nov				Sir Hugh Clifford	
1926	3 Apr	Lord Irwin				

		VICEROY	SECRETARY OF STATE	BURMA	CEYLON	STRAITS SETTLEMENTS
		Irwin	Birkenhead	Butler	Clifford	Guillemard
1927	3 June					Sir Hugh Clifford
	20 Aug				Sir Herbert Stanley	
	20 Dec			Sir Charles Innes		
1928	1 Nov		Lord Peel			
1929	8 June		William Wedgwood Benn			
1930	5 Feb					Sir Cecil Clementi
1931	11 Apr				Sir Graeme Thomson	
	18 Apr	Lord Willingdon				
	26 Aug		Sir Samuel Hoare			
1932	20 Dec			Sir Hugh Stephenson		
1933	23 Dec				Sir Reginald Stubbs	
1934	9 Nov					Sir Shenton Thomas
1935	7 June		Marquess of Zetland			
1936	18 Apr	Marquess of Linlithgow				
	8 May			Commander Sir Archibald Cochrane		
1937	16 Oct				Sir Andrew Caldecott	
1940	15 May		Leopold Amery			
1941	6 May			Sir Reginald Dorman-Smith		
1942	Feb					*Overrun by Japanese Forces*
1943	20 Oct	Field-Marshal Lord Wavell				
1944	4 Dec				Sir Henry Monck-Mason Moore *(Note 22)*	
1945	3 Aug		Lord Pethick-Laurence			
1946	29 Jan					*See next section*
	31 Aug			General Sir Hubert Rance		

		VICEROY	SECRETARY OF STATE	BURMA	CEYLON	STRAITS SETTLEMENTS
		Wavell	Laurence	Rance	Moore	
1947	24 Mar	Admiral Lord Mountbatten *(Note 23)*				
	23 Apr		Lord Listowel *(Note 24)*			

		INDIA	PAKISTAN	BURMA	CEYLON	MALAYSIA	SINGAPORE
1946	29 Jan					Malcolm MacDonald (Note 25)	Sir Franklin Gimson
1947	15 Aug	Admiral Lord Mountbatten	Mohammed Ali Jinnah				
1948	4 Jan			*Sao Shwe Thaik (Note 46)*			
	21 June	Chakravarti Rajagopalachari					
	14 Sept		Khodja Nazim ud-Din				
1949	6 July				Lord Soulbury		
1950	26 Jan	Dr Rajendra Prasad *(Note 46)*					
1951	17 Oct		Ghulam Mohammed				
1952	15 Jan						Sir John Nicholl
	13 Mar			*Dr Ba U*			
1954	17 July				Sir Oliver Goonetilleke		
	22 Dec						Sir Robert Black
1955	16 June					Sir Robert Scott	
	7 Aug		General Iskander Mirza *(Note 26)*				
1957	31 Aug					Tunku Abdul Rahman (Ruler of Negri Sembilan) *(Note 27)*	
	13 Mar			*U Win Maung*			
	9 Dec						Sir William Goode
1958	28 Oct		Field-Marshal Mohammed Ayub Khan				
1959	3 Dec						Inche Yusof bin Ishak
1960	21 Sept					Tunku Syed Putra bin Hassan Jamilullail (Ruler of Perlis)	
1962	2 Mar			*General Ne Win*	William Gopallawa *(Note 28)*		
	13 May	Dr Sarvepalli Radakrishnan					

43

	INDIA	PAKISTAN	BURMA	CEYLON	MALAYSIA	SINGAPORE	BANGLADESH
	Radakrishnan	Ayub Khan	Ne Win	Gopallawa	Jamilullail	bin Ishak	
1965 21 Sept					Tunku Ismail bin Zainal Abidin (Ruler of Trengganu)		
1967 13 May	Dr Zakir Hussain						
1969 31 Mar		General Mohammed Yahya Khan					
24 Aug	Varahgiri Venkata Giri						
1970 21 Sept					Sultan Abdulhalim bin Badlishah (Ruler of Kedah)		
30 Dec						Dr Benjamin Sheares	
1971 24 Dec		Zulficar Ali Bhutto					
1972 12 Jan							Abu Sayeed Chowdury

		INDIA	PAKISTAN	BURMA	CEYLON	MALAYSIA	SINGAPORE
1946	1 Sept	Pandit Jawaharlal Nehru *(Note 29)*					
1947	10 June			*Aung San (Note 30)*			
	19 July		Liaquat Ali Khan				
	20 July			*Thakin Nu (Note 31)*			
	26 Sept				Stephen Senanayake		
1951	17 Oct		Khodja Nazim ud-Din				
1952	26 Mar				Dudley Senanayake		
1953	17 Apr		Mohammed Ali				
	12 Oct				Sir John Kotelawala		
1955	6 Apr						David Marshall
	4 Aug					Tunku Abdul Rahman	
	12 Aug		Chaudry Mohammed Ali				
1956	12 Apr				Solomon Bandaranaike		
	8 June						Lim Yew Hock
	12 June			*U Ba Swe*			
	12 Sept		Husayn Shahid Surawardi				
1957	28 Feb			*U Nu*			
	17 Oct		Ismail Chundrigar				
	16 Dec		Malik Firoz Khan Noon				
1958	24 Oct		General Mohammed Ayub Khan				
	27 Oct		*Post abolished*				
	29 Oct			*General Ne Win*			
1959	9 Feb					Dato Abdul Razak bin Hussein	

		INDIA	PAKISTAN	BURMA	CEYLON	MALAYSIA	SINGAPORE	BANGLADESH
		Nehru	*abolished*	*Ne Win*	Bandaranaike	Abdul Razak	Lim	
1959	5 June						Lee Kuan Yew	
	21 Aug					Tunku Abdul Rahman		
	26 Sept				Wijayananda Dahanayake			
1960	21 Mar				Dudley Senanayake			
	4 Apr			*U Nu*				
	21 July				Mrs Sirimavo Bandaranaike			
1962	2 Mar			*General Ne Win*				
1964	27 May	*Gulzarilal Nanda						
	9 June	Lal Bahadur Shastri						
1965	27 Mar				Dudley Senanayake			
1966	11 Jan	*Gulzarilal Nanda						
	24 Jan	Mrs. Indira Gandhi						
1970	29 May				Mrs Sirimavo Bandaranaike			
	22 Sept					Tun Abdul Razak bin Hussein		
1971	7 Dec		Nurul Amin					
	22 Dec							Tajuddin Ahmed *(Note 32)*
	24 Dec		*None*					
1972	13 Jan							Sheikh Mujibur Rahman

		INDIA	PAKISTAN	BURMA	CEYLON	MALAYSIA	SINGAPORE
1946	1 Sept	Pandit Jawaharlal Nehru *(Note 29)*					
1947	10 June			*Aung San*			
	19 July		Liaquat Ali Khan				
	20 July			*Thakin Nu (Note 31)*			
	2 Aug			*Thakin Lun Baw*			
	26 Sept				Stephen Senanayake		
	31 Oct			*U Tin Tut*			
	28 Dec		Sir Mohammed Zafrullah Khan				
1948	14 Sept			*U Kyaw Nein*			
1949	5 Apr			*U Aye Maung*			
	20 Dec			*Sao Hkun Hkio*			
1952	26 Mar				Dudley Senanayake		
1953	12 Oct				Sir John Kotelawala		
1954	27 Oct		Mohammed Ali				
1955	12 Aug		Chaudry Mohammed Ali				
	26 Sept		Hamidul Huq Chaudry				
1956	12 Apr				Solomon Bandaranaike		
	12 Sept		Malik Firoz Khan Noon				
1957	31 Aug					Tunku Abdul Rahman	
	24 Oct		Manzur Qadir				
	29 Oct			*U Thein Maung*			
1959	9 Feb					Dr Ismail bin Dato Abdul Rahman	
	26 Sept				Wijayananda Dahanayake		
1960	23 Mar				Dudley Senanayake		

		INDIA	PAKISTAN	BURMA	CEYLON	MALAYSIA	SINGAPORE
		Nehru	Qadir	Maung	Senanayake	Ismail	
1960	4 Apr			*Sao Hkun Hkio*			
	23 July				Mrs Sirimavo Bandaranaike		
	18 Aug					Tunku Abdul Rahman	
1962	2 Mar			*U Thi Han*			
	13 June		Mohammed Ali				
1963	24 Jan		Zulficar Ali Bhutto				
1964	27 May	*Vacant*					
	9 June	Lal Bahadur Shastri					
	20 July	Sardar Swaran Singh					
1965	27 Mar				Dudley Senanayake		
	9 Aug						Sinathamby Rajaratnam
1966	18 June		*Field-Marshal Mohammed Ayub Khan				
	20 July		Shariffidin Pirzada				
	13 Nov	Mohammedan Currim Chagla					
1967	5 Sept	Mrs Indira Gandhi					
1968	24 Apr		Arshad Husain				
1969	14 Feb	Dinesh Singh					
	3 Mar		President Yahya Khan *(Note 33)*				
	19 June			*Colonel Maung Lwin*			
1970	29 May				Mrs Sirimavo Bandaranaike		
	27 June	Sardar Swaran Singh					
	4 Aug			Hla Han			
	23 Sept					Tun Abdul Razak bin Hussein	
1971	21 Feb		*None (Note 34)*				

		INDIA	PAKISTAN	BURMA	CEYLON	MALAYSIA	SINGAPORE	BANGLADESH
		Swaran Singh	*None*	*Lwin*	Bandaranaike	Abdul Razak	Rajaratnam	
1971	7 Dec		Zulficar Ali Bhutto					
	22 Dec							Abdus Samad Azad *(Note 32)*
1972	20 Apr			*U Kyaw Soe*				

		INDIA	PAKISTAN	BURMA	CEYLON	MALAYSIA	SINGAPORE
1946	1 Sept	Sardar Baldev Singh *(Note 29)*					
1947	10 June			*Aung San*			
	19 July		Liaquat Ali Khan				
	20 July			*Colonel Bo Let Yar*			
	26 Sept				Stephen Senanayake		
1948	14 Sept			*Thakin Nu (Note 31)*			
1949	5 Apr			*General Ne Win*			
1950	11 Sept			*U Win*			
1951	23 Oct		Khodja Nazim ud-Din				
1952	16 Mar			*U Ba Swe*			
	26 Mar				Dudley Senanayake		
	13 May	Sir Gopalaswami Ayyangar					
1953	10 Feb	Pandit Jawaharlal Nehru					
	15 Mar	Mahavir Tyagi					
	17 Apr		Mohammed Ali				
	12 Oct				Sir John Kotelawala		
1954	27 Oct		General Mohammed Ayub Khan				
	7 Dec	Pandit Jawaharlal Nehru					
1955	10 Jan	Dr Kailas Nath Katju					
	12 Aug		Chaudry Mohammed Ali				
1956	12 Apr				Solomon Bandaranaike		
	12 Sept		Husayn Shahid Surawardi				
1957	30 Jan	Pandit Jawaharlal Nehru					
	17 Apr	Vengalil Krishna Menon					

51

		INDIA	PAKISTAN	BURMA	CEYLON	MALAYSIA	SINGAPORE
		Menon	Surawardi	*Swe*	Bandaranaike		
1957	31 Aug					Dato Abdul Razak bin Hussein	
	17 Oct		Mian Mumtaz Mohammed Khan Daulana				
	16 Dec		Malik Firoz Khan Noon				
1958	8 Apr		Mohammed Ayub Khusro				
	16 July			*Bo Hmu Aung*			
	29 Oct			*General Ne Win*			
	24 Oct		General Mohammed Ayub Khan				
1959	26 Sept				Wijayananda Dahanayake		
1960	21 Mar				Dudley Senanayake		
	4 Apr			*U Nu*			
	23 July				Mrs Sirimavo Bandaranaike		
1962	2 Mar			*General Ne Win*			
	31 Oct	Pandit Jawaharlal Nehru					
	14 Nov	Yashwantrao Chavan					
1965	27 Mar				Dudley Senanayake		
	9 Aug						Dr Goh Keng Swee
1966	7 Oct		Admiral Afzal Rahman Khan				
	13 Nov	Sardar Swaran Singh					
1967	17 Aug						Lim Kin San
1969	3 Mar		President Yahya Khan *(Note 33)*				
1970	29 May				Mrs Sirimavo Bandaranaike		

		INDIA	PAKISTAN	BURMA	CEYLON	MALAYSIA	SINGAPORE	BANGLADESH
		Swaran Singh	Khan	*Ne Win*	Bandaranaike	Abdul Razak	Lim	
1970	27 June	Jagjivan Ram						
	11 Aug						Dr Goh Keng Swee	
1971	21 Feb		*None (Note 34)*					
	22 Dec							Tajuddin Ahmed *(Note 32)*
	24 Dec		Zulficar Ali Bhutto					
1972	13 Jan							Sheikh Mujibur Rahman
	20 Apr			*General San Yu*				

	INDIA	PAKISTAN	BURMA	CEYLON	MALAYSIA	SINGAPORE
1946 1 Sept	Sardar Vallabhai Patel (Note 29)					
1947 10 June			*U Kyaw Nein*			
19 July		Ghazanfar Ali Khan				
15 Aug		Fazlur Rahman				
26 Sept				Sir Oliver Goonetilleke		
1948 10 May		Khodja Shahbuddin				
22 July				E.A.P. Wijeratne		
14 Sept			*Thakin Nu (Note 31)*			
1949 5 Apr			*General Ne Win*			
1950 11 Sept			*U Win*			
26 Dec	Chakravarti Rajagopalachari					
1951 1 Mar				Sir Oliver Goonetilleke		
25 Oct	Dr Kailas Nath Katju					
20 Nov		Mushtaq Ahmed Gurmani				
1952 16 Mar			*Bo Khin Maung Gale*			
2 June				C.A. Ratnayake		
1954 27 Oct		General Iskander Mirza				
1955 10 Jan	Pandit Govind Pant					
12 Aug		Fazlul Huq				
4 Aug					Tunku Abdul Rahman	
1956 12 Apr				Alexander Perera Jayasuria		
12 June			*Thakin Tha Khin*			
12 Sept		Mir Ghulam Ali Talpur				
1957 31 Aug					Inche Suleiman bin Dato Abdul Rahman	

Date	INDIA	PAKISTAN	BURMA	CEYLON	MALAYSIA	SINGAPORE
	Pant	Talpur	*Tha Khin*	Jayasuria	Suleiman	
1958 7 Apr		Khan Mohammed Jalaluddin Khan				
25 Apr			*Bo Min Gaung*			
24 Oct		General Khalid Sheikh				
29 Oct			*U Khin Maung Hpyu*			
1959 5 June						Ong Pang Boon *(Note 35)*
9 June				Tikiri Ilangaratne		
8 Dec				Stanley de Zoysa		
1960 23 Mar				Dr M.C.M. Kaleel		
4 Apr			*U Nu*			
June		Zakir Hussein				
23 July				Maithripala Senanayake		
1961 4 Apr	Lal Bahadur Shastri					
1962 2 Mar			*Colonel Kyaw Soe*			
13 June		Habibullah Khan				
1963 29 May				Alexander Perera Jayasuria		
29 Aug	Gulzarilal Nanda					
1964 2 May					Dato Ismail bin Dato Abdul Rahman	
1965 27 Mar				Wijayananda Dahanayake		
29 Mar		*None announced*				
17 Aug		Ali Akhbar Khan				
1966 13 Nov	Yashwantrao Chavan					
1967 Feb					Tun Abdul Razak bin Hussein	
1969 3 Mar		*None (Note 34)*				
21 May					Dato Ismail bin Dato Abdul Rahman	

	INDIA	PAKISTAN	BURMA	CEYLON	MALAYSIA	SINGAPORE	BANGLADESH
	Chavan	*None*	*Kyaw Soe*	Dahanayake	Ismail	Ong	
1969 4 Aug		Sardar Abdul Rashid					
1970 31 May				Felix Dias Bandaranaike			
27 June	Mrs Indira Gandhi						
6 Sept						Professor Wong Lin Ken	
1971 21 Feb		*None* *(Note 34)*					
22 Dec							A. H. M. Kamaruzzam *(Note 32)*
24 Dec		Zulficar Ali Bhutto					
1972 13 Jan							Sheikh Mujibur Rahman
18 Apr		*Khan Abdul Qayyum Khan*					
20 Apr			*U Sein Mya*				
10 Sept						E. W. Barrow	
22 Sept			*U Ko Ko*				
1 Nov						Choa Sian-Chin	

	INDIA	PAKISTAN	BURMA	CEYLON	MALAYSIA	SINGAPORE
1946 1 Sept	John Matthaei *(Note 36)*					
26 Oct	Liaquat Ali Khan *(Note 36)*					
1947 10 June			*Thakin Mya*			
19 July	Chakravarti Rajagopala- chari	Liaquat Ali Khan				
20 July			*Thakin Lun Baw*			
2 Aug			*U Tin Tut*			
15 Aug	Shanmukham Chatty	Ghulam Mohammed				
26 Sept				J. R. Jayawardene		
18 Nov			*U Ko Gyi*			
1948 1 Mar			*U Tin*			
16 Aug	*K. C. Neogy					
22 Sept	John Matthaei					
1950 25 May	Sir Chintaman Desmukh					
1951 27 Oct		Chaudry Mohammed Ali				
1953 13 Oct				Sir Oliver Goonetilleke		
1954 27 June				M. D. H. Jayawardene		
1955 17 Oct		Syed Amjad Ali				
1956 12 Apr				Stanley de Zoysa		
12 June			*Bo Khin Maung Gale*			
24 July	Pandit Jawaharlal Nehru					
1 Sept	T. T. Krishnamachari					
1957 31 Aug					Sir Henry Hau-Shik Lee	
1958 13 Feb	Pandit Jawaharlal Nehru					
13 Mar	Morarji Desai					
4 June			*U Kyaw Nein*			

	INDIA	PAKISTAN	BURMA	CEYLON	MALAYSIA	SINGAPORE
	Desai	Ali	*Nein*	de Zoysa	Lee	
1958 24 Oct		Dr Mohammed Shoaib				
1959 5 June						Dr Goh Keng-Swee
22 Aug					Tan Siew Sin	
22 Nov				Mohammed Mustafa		
1960 23 Mar				J. R. Jayawardene		
4 Apr			*Thakin Tin*			
21 July				Felix Dias Bandaranaike		
1962 30 Jan		Abdul Qadir				
2 Mar			*General Ne Win*			
27 Aug				C. P. de Silva		
8 Nov				Idamptiya Kalugalla		
14 Dec		Dr Mohammed Shoaib				
1963 29 May				Tikiri Illangaratne		
29 Aug	T. T. Krishnamachari					
3 Dec			*Brigadier San Yu*			
1964 11 June				Dr Nanayakkarapathirage Martin Perera		
1965 27 Mar				U. B. Wanninayake		
9 Aug						Lim Kin-San
31 Dec	Sachinda Chauduri					
1966 25 Aug		Nabi Uqaili				
1967 13 Mar	Morarji Desai					
17 Aug						Dr Goh Keng-Swee
1969 3 Mar		None *(Note 34)*				
21 May					*Tun Abdul Razak bin Hussein	
16 July	Mrs Indira Gandhi					

		INDIA	PAKISTAN	BURMA	CEYLON	MALAYSIA	SINGAPORE	BANGLADESH
		Gandhi	*None*	*San Yu*	Wanninayake	Abdul Razak	Goh	
1969	4 Aug		Nawab Mozaffer Ali Qizilbashi					
1970	31 May				Dr Nanayakkarapathirage Martin Perera			
	27 June	Yashwantrao Chavan						
	11 Aug						Hon Sui-Sec	
	23 Sept					Tan Siew Sin		
1971	21 Feb		None *(Note 34)*					
	24 Dec		Dr Mubashir Hasan					
	22 Dec							Mansoor Ali *(Note 32)*
1972	13 Jan							Tajuddin Ahmed
	20 Apr			*U Lwin*				

		GIBRALTAR	MALTA	CYPRUS	PALESTINE
1900	1 Jan	General Sir Robert Biddulph	General Sir Francis Grenfell	Sir William Haynes-Smith	
	10 July	Field-Marshal Sir George White V.C.			
1903	2 Apr		General Sir Charles Mansfield Clarke		
1904	17 Oct			Sir Charles King-Harman	
1905	5 Sept	General Sir Frederick Forestier-Walker			
1907	5 Aug		General Sir Henry Fane Grant		
1909	30 Sept		General Sir Henry Rundle		
1910	4 Oct	General Sir Archibald Hunter			
1911	12 Oct			Sir Hamilton John Goold-Adams	
1913	11 July	General Sir Herbert Miles			
1915	8 Jan			Sir John Clausen	
	14 Feb		Field-Marshal Lord Methuen		
1918	7 Sept	General Sir Horace Smith-Dorrien			
1919	11 June		Field-Marshal Lord Plumer		
1920	1 July				Sir Herbert Samuel
	31 July			Sir Malcolm Stevenson *(Note 37)*	
1923	18 Sept	General Sir Charles Monro			
1924	29 June		General Sir Walter Norris Congreve V.C.		
1925	25 Aug				Field-Marshal Lord Plumer

	GIBRALTAR	MALTA	CYPRUS	PALESTINE
	Monro	Congreve	Stevenson	Plumer
1926 30 Nov			Sir Ronald Storrs	
1927 9 May		General Sir John Du Cane		
1928 16 Oct	General Sir Alexander Godley			
6 Dec				Sir John Chancellor
1931 5 Oct		General Sir David Campbell		
20 Nov				General Sir Arthur Wauchope
1932 21 Nov			Sir Edward Stubbs	
1933 24 Oct	General Sir Charles Harington			
9 Dec			Sir Herbert Palmer Richmond	
1936 6 Apr		General Sir Charles Bonham-Carter		
1938 3 Mar				Sir Harold MacMichael
9 Nov	General Sir Edmund Ironside			
1939 11 July	General Sir Clive Liddell			
10 Aug			Sir William Battershill	
1940 14 Oct		General Sir William Dobbie		
1941 14 May	General Lord Gort V.C.			
25 Nov			Sir Charles Campbell Woolley	
1942 11 May		Field-Marshal Lord Gort V.C.		
19 June	General Sir Noel Mason-MacFarlane			
1944 27 Feb	General Sir Ralph Eastwood			

	GIBRALTAR	MALTA	CYPRUS	PALESTINE/ ISRAEL
	Eastwood	Gort	Woolley	MacMichael
1944 19 July				Field-Marshal Lord Gort V. C.
27 Sept		General Sir Edmond Schreiber		
1945 8 Nov				General Sir Alan Cunningham
1946 10 July		Sir Francis Douglas		
1947 21 Mar	General Sir Kenneth Anderson			
27 Mar			Lord Winster	
1948 14 May				*End of Mandate*
16 May				*Dr Chaim Weizmann*
1949 4 Aug			Sir Andrew Wright	
16 Sept		Sir Gerald Creasy		
1952 9 May	General Sir Gordon MacMillan			
8 Dec				*Izhak Ben Zvi*
1954 19 Feb			Sir Robert Armitage	
20 Sept		General Sir Robert Laycock		
1955 20 May	General Sir Harold Redman			
3 Oct			Field-Marshal Sir John Harding	
1957 3 Dec			Sir Hugh Foot	
1958 24 May	General Sir Charles Keighley			
1959 8 June		Admiral Sir Guy Grantham		
1960 16 Aug			Archbishop Makarios *(Note 46)*	
1962 2 July		Sir Maurice Dorman		
31 July	General Sir Dudley Ward			

	GIBRALTAR	MALTA	CYPRUS	PALESTINE/ ISRAEL
	Ward	Dorman	Makarios	*Ben Zvi*
1963 21 May				*Schneor Zalman Shazar*
1965 28 Aug	General Sir Gerald Lathbury			
1969 17 Apr	Admiral of the Fleet Sir Varyl Begg			
1971 5 July		Sir Anthony Mamo		

	GIBRALTAR	MALTA	CYPRUS	ISRAEL
1947 4 Nov		Dr Paul Boffa		
1948 14 May				*David Ben Gurion*
1950 17 Sept		Dr Enrico Mizzi		
20 Dec		Dr Borg Olivier		
1953 9 Dec				*Moshe Sharett*
1955 10 Mar		Dom Mintoff		
2 Nov				*David Ben Gurion*
1958 30 Apr		*Constitution suspended*		
1959 5 Apr			Archbishop Makarios	
1960 16 Aug			*None (Note 38)*	
1962 5 Mar		Dr Borg Olivier		
1963 24 June				*Levi Eshkol*
1964 11 Aug	Sir Joshua Hassan			
1969 3 Mar				*Mrs Golda Meir*
6 Aug	Major Robert Peliza			
1971 21 June		Dom Mintoff		

	GIBRALTAR	MALTA	CYPRUS	ISRAEL
1948 14 May				*Moshe Sharett (Shertok)*
1956 18 June				*Mrs Golda Meir (Myerson)*
1959 5 Apr			Archbishop Makarios	
1960 22 Aug			Spyros Kyprianou	
1964 21 Sept		Dr Borg Olivier		
1966 10 Jan				*Abba Eban*
1971 21 June		Dom Mintoff		
1972 16 June			Ioannis Khristofidhis	

	GIBRALTAR	MALTA	CYPRUS	ISRAEL
1948 14 May				*David Ben Gurion*
1954 4 Jan				*Pinhas Lavon*
1955 17 Feb				*David Ben Gurion*
1959 5 Apr			Osman Orek	
1963 24 June				*Levi Eshkol*
1966 20 Apr			Polycarpos Georghadjis *(Note 39)*	
1967 1 June				*General Moshe Dayan*
1968 10 Dec			Epaminondas Komodromos	
1972 16 June			Georgios Ioannides	

	GIBRALTAR	MALTA	CYPRUS	ISRAEL
1948 14 May				*Isaac Gruenbaum*
1949 3 Mar				*Moshe Shapira*
1952 22 Dec				*Israel Rokach*
1955 29 June				*Moshe Shapira*
2 Nov				*Israel Bar-Yehuda*
1959 5 Apr			Tassos Papadopoulos	
16 Dec				*Moshe Shapira*
1960 14 Aug			Polycarpos Georghadjis	
1968 9 Dec			Epaminondas Komodromos	
1970 1 Sept				*Yosef Berg*
1972 16 June			Georgios Ioannides	

		GIBRALTAR	MALTA	CYPRUS	ISRAEL
1947	4 Nov		Dr A Colombo		
1948	14 May				*Eliezer Kaplan*
1950	26 Sept		Dr Frendo Azzopardi		
1952	25 June				*Levi Eshkol*
1955	10 Mar		Dom Mintoff		
1958	30 Apr		*Constitution suspended*		
1959	5 Apr			Righinos Theocarous	
1962	5 Mar		Dr Borg Olivier		
	1 July			Renos Solomides	
1963	24 June				*Pinhas Sapir*
1968	15 June			Andreas Patsalides	
	26 July				*Zeev Sharef*
1969	15 Dec				*Pinhas Sapir*
1971	21 June		Dr Joseph Abela		

	NIGERIA	GOLD COAST	GAMBIA	SIERRA LEONE	KENYA	UGANDA	TANGANYIKA
1900 1 Jan		Sir Frederick Hodgson	Sir Robert Llewelyn	Colonel Sir Frederick Cardew		Sir Harry Johnston	
11 Dec				Sir Charles King-Harman			
17 Dec		Sir Matthew Nathan					
1901 11 Jan			Sir George Denton *(Note 40)*				
Dec						Colonel Sir James Hayes Sadler	
1904 3 Mar		Sir John Rodger					
3 Oct				Sir Leslie Probyn			
1905 31 Dec					Colonel Sir James Hayes Sadler		
1907 20 Nov						Sir Hesketh Bell *(Note 41)*	
1909 16 Sept					Sir Percy Girouard		
1910 1 Feb						Captain Harry Cordeaux	
21 Nov		James Thorburn					
1911 3 Apr						Sir Frederick Jackson	
29 Apr				Sir Edward Mereweather			
21 Dec			Colonel Sir Henry Galway				
1912 3 Oct					Sir Henry Belfield		
26 Dec		Sir Hugh Clifford					
1914 1 Jan	Sir Frederick Lugard *(Note 42)*						
11 Apr			Sir Edward Cameron				
1916 9 Mar				Richard James Wilkinson			
23 Sept							Sir Horace Byatt
1918 10 Feb						Sir Robert Coryndon	

	NIGERIA	GOLD COAST	GAMBIA	SIERRA LEONE	KENYA	UGANDA	TANGANYIKA
	Lugard	Clifford	Cameron	Wilkinson	Belfield	Coryndon	Byatt
1919 31 Jan					General Sir Edward Northey		
8 Aug	Sir Hugh Clifford						
7 Oct		Brigadier-General Sir Gordon Guggisberg					
1921 3 Jan			Sir Cecil Armitage				
1922 4 May				Sir Alexander Ransford Slater			
15 Aug					Sir Robert Coryndon	Sir Geoffrey Archer	
1925 3 Apr							Sir Donald Cameron
18 May						Sir William Frederick Gowers	
2 Oct					Sir Edward Grigg		
13 Nov	Sir Graeme Thomson						
1927 10 Mar			Sir John Middleton				
20 July		Sir Alexander Ransford Slater					
24 Sept				Brigadier-General Sir Joseph Byrne			
1928 29 Nov			Sir Edward Denham				
1930 11 Sept			Sir Richmond Palmer				
1931 13 Feb					Brigadier-General Sir Joseph Byrne		
23 May				Sir Arnold Hodson			Sir George Stewart Symes
17 June	Sir Donald Cameron						
1932 20 May		Sir Shenton Thomas					
23 Nov						Sir Bernard Henry Bourdillon	
1934 19 Feb							Sir Harold MacMichael
12 Apr			Sir Arthur Richards				
24 Oct		Sir Arnold Hodson					

	NIGERIA	GOLD COAST	GAMBIA	SIERRA LEONE	KENYA	UGANDA	TANGANYIKA
	Cameron	Hodson	Richards	Hodson	Byrne	Bourdillon	MacMichael
1934 8 Dec				Sir Henry Monck-Mason Moore			
1935 17 Oct						Sir Philip Mitchell	
1 Nov	Sir Bernard Henry Bourdillon						
1936 22 Oct			Sir Thomas Southorn				
1937 6 Apr					Air Chief Marshal Sir Robert Brooke-Popham		
13 Nov				Sir Douglas Jardine			
1938 8 July							Sir Mark Young
1940 9 Jan					Sir Henry Monck-Mason Moore		
7 July						Sir Charles Dundas	
1941 15 Aug				Sir Hubert Stevenson			
6 Nov		Sir Alan Burns					
1942 17 Mar							Sir Wilfrid Jackson
23 Mar			Sir Hilary Blood				
1943 18 Dec	Sir Arthur Richards						
1944 11 Dec					Sir Philip Mitchell		
1945 1 Jan						Sir John Hathorn Hall	
5 May							Sir William Battershill
1947 29 Mar			Sir Andrew Wright				
14 Apr	Sir John Macpherson (Note 43)						
1948 13 Jan		Sir Gerald Creasy					
4 Sept				Sir George Beresford-Stooke			
1949 18 June							Sir Edward Twining
12 Aug		Sir Charles Arden-Clarke (Note 44)					
1 Dec			Sir Percy Wyn-Harris				

	NIGERIA	GOLD COAST	GAMBIA	SIERRA LEONE	KENYA	UGANDA	TANGANYIKA
	Macpherson	Arden-Clarke	Wyn-Harris	Stooke	Mitchell	Hall	Twining
1952 17 Jan						Sir Andrew Cohen	
30 Sept					Sir Evelyn Baring		
1953 18 Apr				Sir Robert de Zouche Hall			
1955 15 June	Sir James Robertson						
1956 1 Sept				Sir Maurice Dorman			
1957 26 Feb						Sir Frederick Crawford	
24 June		Earl of Listowel					
1958 19 June			Sir Edward Windley				
15 July							Sir Richard Turnbull *(Note 45)*
1959 23 Oct					Sir Patrick Renison		
1960 1 July		Dr Kwame Nkrumah *(Note 46)*					
16 Nov	Dr Nnamdi Azikiwe *(Note 47)*						
1961 19 Nov						Sir Walter Coutts *(Note 48)*	
1962 29 Mar			Sir John Warburton Paul *(Note 49)*				
27 Apr				Sir Henry Lightfoot Boston			
9 Dec							Dr Julius Nyerere *(Note 50)*
1963 4 Jan					Malcolm MacDonald *(Note 51)*		
9 Oct						Sir Edward Mutesa II Kabaka of Buganda *(Note 46)*	
1964 12 Dec					Jomo Kenyatta *(Note 46)*		
1966 21 Jan	General Johnson Aguiyi-Ironsi *(Note 52)*						

		NIGERIA	GHANA	GAMBIA	SIERRA LEONE	KENYA	UGANDA	TANZANIA
		Ironsi	Nkrumah	Paul	Boston	Kenyatta	Buganda	Nyerere
1966	18 Feb			Alhaji Sir Farimang Singhateh				
	24 Feb		General Joseph Arthur Ankrah *(Note 53)*					
	10 Mar						*Presidency abolished*	
	15 Apr						Dr Apollo Milton Obote	
	1 Aug	General Yakubu Gowon *(Note 54)*						
1967	27 Mar				Colonel Andrew Juxon-Smith *(Note 55)*			
1968	22 Apr				*Chief Justice Banjo Tejansie			
1969	2 Apr		Brigadier Akwasi Amankawa Afrifa					
1970	24 Apr			Sir Dauda Jawara *(Note 46)*				
	28 Aug		Edward Akufo-Addo					
1971	25 Jan						General Idi Amin (Dada)	
	31 Mar				Justice Christopher Okoro Cole			
	21 Apr				Siaka Probyn Stevens *(Note 46)*			
1972	29 Jan		Colonel Ignatius Kutu Acheampong *(Note 56)*					

PRIME MINISTERS

		NIGERIA	GHANA	GAMBIA	SIERRA LEONE	KENYA	UGANDA	TANGANYIKA
1952	5 Mar		Dr Kwame Nkrumah					
1954	9 July				Sir Milton Margai			
1957	30 Aug	Alhaji Sir Abubakar Tafawa Balewa *(Note 57)*						
1960	1 July		*None (Note 38)*					
	2 Sept							Dr Julius Nyerere
1961	22 Mar			Pierre N'jie				
	2 July						Benedicto Kiwanuka	
1962	22 Jan							Rashidi Kawawa
	6 Apr					Jomo Kenyatta *(Note 58)*		
	30 Apr						Dr Apollo Milton Obote	
	4 June			Sir Dauda Jawara				
	9 Dec							*Post abolished*
1964	28 Apr				Sir Albert Margai			
	12 Dec					*None (Note 38)*		
1966	16 Jan	*None (Note 59)*						
	15 Apr						*None (Note 38)*	
1967	21 Mar				Siaka Probyn Stevens			
	26 Mar				*None (Note 59)*			
1968	26 Apr				Siaka Probyn Stevens			
1969	3 Sept		Dr Kofi Busia					
1970	24 Apr			*None (Note 38)*				
1971	21 Apr				Sorie Ibrahim Koroma			
1972	29 Jan		*None (Note 59)*					
	17 Feb							Rashidi Kawawa

	NIGERIA	GHANA	GAMBIA	SIERRA LEONE	KENYA	UGANDA	TANZANIA
	None	*None*	Jawara	Kallon	Koinange	Odaka	Nyerere
1966 19 June		General Joseph Arthur Ankrah					
1 Aug	General Yakubu Gowon						
1967 5 Jan					James Nyamweya		
13 Mar		John Willie Kofi Harlley					
19 Mar			Alhaji A. B. N'jie				
30 Mar				William Leigh			
3 Sept	Dr Okoi Arikpo						
30 Dec			Sheriff Sekuba Sisay				
1968 4 Jan			Andrew Camara		C. M. G. Argwings-Kodhek		
1969 14 Feb		Patrick Anin					
26 Apr				L. A. M. Brewah			
5 Feb					Mbiyu Koinange		
9 Apr		Victor Owusu					
11 Apr				Cyril Foray			
15 Apr		Patrick Anin					
7 Sept		Victor Owusu					
22 Dec					Dr Njoroge Mungai		
1970 5 Nov							Israel Elinawings
1971 28 Jan		William Ofori-Atta					
3 Feb						Wanume Kibedi	
21 Apr				Solomon Pratt			
1972 29 Jan		General Nathan Aferi					

		NIGERIA	GHANA	GAMBIA	SIERRA LEONE	KENYA	UGANDA	TANZANIA
		Arikpo	Aferi	Camara	Pratt	Mungai	Kibedi	Elinawings
1972	17 Feb							John Malecela
	18 Oct		Major Kwame Baah					

		NIGERIA	GHANA	GAMBIA	SIERRA LEONE	KENYA	UGANDA	TANGANYIKA
1957	6 Mar		Dr Kwame Nkrumah					
1960	1 July		Charles de Graft Dickson					
	1 Oct	Alhaji Muhammadu Ribadu						
1961	27 Apr				Sir Milton Margai			
	30 Sept		Kofi Baako					
1962	30 Apr						Dr Apollo Milton Obote	
1963	1 June					Jomo Kenyatta		
1964	29 Apr				Sir Albert Margai			
	10 Dec					Dr Njoroge Mungai		
1965	13 Mar			Sir Dauda Jawara				
	23 May	Alhaji Inuwa Wada					Felix Kenyi Onama	
1966	21 Jan	*None*						
	24 Feb		*None*					
	19 June		General Emmanuel Kwasi Kotoka					
	1 Aug	General Yakubu Gowon						
1967	27 Mar				Colonel Andrew Juxon-Smith			
	1 July		General Joseph Arthur Ankrah					
1968	26 Apr				Siaka Probyn Stevens			
1969	9 Apr		General Albert Kwesi Okran					
	7 Sept		J. Kwesi-Lamptey					
	22 Dec					James Gichuru		
1971	28 Jan		Bukari Adama					

		NIGERIA	GHANA	GAMBIA	SIERRA LEONE	KENYA	UGANDA	TANZANIA
		Gowon	Adama	Jawara	Stevens	Gichuru	Onama	
1971	2 Feb						General Idi Amin (Dada)	
	16 June						Charles Oboth-Ofumbi	
1972	29 Jan		Colonel Ignatius Kutu Acheampong					
	17 Feb							Edward Sokoine *(Note 63)*

	NIGERIA	GHANA	GAMBIA	SIERRA LEONE	KENYA	UGANDA	TANGANYIKA
1954 17 June		Archie Casely-Hayford					
1956 19 May		Ako Adjei					
1957 29 Aug		Krobo Edusei					
30 Aug	Joseph Modupe Johnson						
1958 14 Aug				Sir Milton Margai			
17 Nov		Dr Kwame Nkrumah					
1959 1 July		Ashford Emmanuel Inksumah					
23 Dec	Mallam Usman Sarki						
1960 2 Sept							Clement George Kahama
1961 30 Sept		Kwaku Boateng					
1962 22 Jan							Oscar Kambona
1 Mar						G. O. B. Oda	
30 Apr						William Wilberforce Nadiope	
4 June			Sheriff Dibba (Note 64)				
9 Oct						Felix Kenyi Onama	
7 Dec	Alhaji Shehu Shegari						
1963 12 Mar							Job Lusinde
1 June					Oginga Odinga		
1964 29 Apr				Maglore Kallon			
1 May		Lawrence Rosario Abavana					
10 Dec					Daniel Arap Moi		
1965 24 Jan		Ashford Emmanuel Inksumah					
23 May	Alhaji Ali Mungoro					Basil Bataringaya	

	NIGERIA	GHANA	GAMBIA	SIERRA LEONE	KENYA	UGANDA	TANZANIA
	Mungoro	Inksumah	*Dibba*	Kallon	Moi	Bataringaya	Lusinde
1965 12 June		Lawrence Rosario Abavana					
30 Sept							Lawi Sijaona
23 Nov				Ahmed Wurie			
1966 21 Jan	*None*						
24 Feb		*None*					
2 June			B. L. K. Sanyang				
19 June		John Willie Kofi Harlley					
1967 30 Mar				Colonel Andrew Juxon-Smith			
7 June							Saidi Maswanya
12 June	Alhaji Kam Selem						
30 Dec			Alioune Badara N'diaye				
1968 26 Apr				Sahr Washingtoncava Gandi Capio			
1969 11 Apr				Siaka Probyn Stevens			
30 May			Yaya Ceesay				
7 Sept		Simeon Deodong Dombo					
1971 28 Jan		Nicholas Yaw Boafo Adade					
2 Feb						Colonel E. A. T. Obitre Gama	
21 Apr				Sheku Bokhari Kawasu-Konteh			
1972 29 Jan		J. H. Cobbina					
Feb				Sorie Ibrahim Koroma			
Spring						General Idi Amin (Dada)	

MINISTERS OF FINANCE

	NIGERIA	GHANA	GAMBIA	SIERRA LEONE	KENYA	UGANDA	TANGANYIKA
1954 17 June		Komlah Agbeli Gbedemah					
1957 30 Aug	Alhaji Sir Abubakar Tafawa Balewa						
17 Sept	Chief Festus Okotie-Eboh						
1958 14 Aug				Mohammed Sanusi Mustapha			
1960 2 Sept							Sir Ernest Vasey
1961 8 May		Ferdinand Koblavi Dra Goka					
1962 22 Jan							Paul Bomani
1 Mar						Lawrence Sebalu	
6 Apr					James Gichuru		
30 Apr						Amos Kalule Sempa	
4 June			Sheriff Sekuba Sisay				
5 June		—		Dr Albert Margai			
1964 19 Feb		Dr Kwame Nkrumah					
29 Apr				Robert Granville Jumeri King			
1 May		Kwesi Amoaka-Atta					
2 Oct						Lawrence Kalule-Settaala	
1965 30 Sept							Amir Jamal
1966 21 Jan	*None*						
24 Feb		*None*					
19 June		Brigadier Akwasi Amankawa Afrifa					
1967 30 Mar				Colonel Andrew Juxon-Smith			

	NIGERIA	GHANA	GAMBIA	SIERRA LEONE	KENYA	UGANDA	TANZANIA
	None	Afrifa	Sisay	Smith	Gichuru	Settaala	Jamal
1967 2 June	Chief Awolowo						
30 Dec			Sheriff Dibba				
1968 26 Apr				Dr Mohammed Sorie Forna			
1969 9 Apr		John Mensah					
22 Dec					Mwai Kibaki		
1970 14 Sept				A. G. Sembu Forna			
1971 2 Feb						Emmanuel Wakhweya	
21 Apr				Christian Alusine Kamara-Taylor			
14 Oct	Alhaji Shehu Shagari						
1972 29 Jan		Colonel Ignatius Kutu Acheampong					
17 Feb							Cleopa Msuya
9 Oct			Ibrahim Garba Jahumpa				

GOVERNORS/GOVERNORS-GENERAL/HIGH COMMISSIONERS/HEADS OF STATE

	MAURITIUS	NYASALAND	NORTHERN RHODESIA	HIGH COMMISSIONER FOR BRITISH SOUTH AFRICA
1900 1 Jan	Sir Charles Bruce			
1904 20 Aug	Sir Cavendish Boyle			
1907 Oct		*Brigadier-General Sir William Manning		
1908 Apr		Sir Alfred Sharpe		
1910 Apr		*Major Francis Pearce		
4 July		*Henry Wallis		
1911 6 Feb		Brigadier-General Sir William Manning		
13 Nov	Sir John Chancellor			
1912 Dec		*Major Francis Pearce		
1913 23 Sept		Sir George Smith		
1916 18 May	Sir Hesketh Bell			
1924 27 Mar		Sir Charles Bowring		
1 Apr			Sir Herbert Stanley	
1925 19 Feb	Sir Herbert Read			
1927 31 Aug			Sir James Maxwell	
1929 7 Nov		Sir Shenton Thomas		
1930 30 Aug	Sir Wilfrid Jackson			
1931 6 Apr				Sir Herbert Stanley
1932 22 Nov		Sir Hubert Young		
1 Dec			Sir Ronald Storrs	
1934 20 Mar			Sir Hubert Young	
21 Sept		Sir Harold Kittermaster		
1935 7 Jan				Sir William Clark
1937 21 Oct	Sir Bede Clifford			
1938 1 Sept			Sir John Maybin	

	MAURITIUS	NYASALAND (MALAWI)	NORTHERN RHODESIA (ZAMBIA)	HIGH COMMISSIONER FOR BRITISH SOUTH AFRICA
	Clifford	Kittermaster	Maybin	Clark
1939 20 Mar		Sir Henry Mackenzie-Kennedy		
1940 6 Jan				Sir Edward Harding
1941 22 Feb				Lord Harlech
16 Oct			Sir Eubule John Waddington	
1942 5 July	Sir Henry Mackenzie-Kennedy			
8 Aug		Sir Edmund Richards		
1944 27 Oct				Sir Evelyn Baring
1948 19 Feb			Sir Gilbert Rennie	
30 Mar		Sir Geoffrey Colby		
1949 26 Sept	Sir Hilary Blood			
1951 2 Oct				Sir John Le Rougetel
1954 22 Mar	Sir Robert Scott			
25 Apr			Sir Arthur Benson	
1955 4 Mar				Sir Percivale Liesching
1956 10 Apr		Sir Robert Armitage		
1959 15 Jan				Sir John Maud
22 Apr			Sir Evelyn Hone	
3 Nov	Sir Colville Deverell			
1961 10 Apr		Sir Glyn Jones		
1962 17 Sept	Sir John Shaw Rennie			
1963 6 June				Sir Hugh Stephenson
1964 1 Aug				*Post abolished See next page*
24 Oct			Kenneth Kaunda *(Note 46)*	
1966 6 July		Dr Hastings Banda *(Note 46)*		
1968 3 Sept	Sir Leonard Williams			

		LESOTHO	BOTSWANA	SWAZILAND
1966	30 Sept		Sir Seretse Khama	
	4 Oct	Moeshoeshoe II *(Note 65)*		
1968	6 Sept			Sobhuza II *(Note 66)*

	MAURITIUS	MALAWI	ZAMBIA	LESOTHO	BOTSWANA	SWAZILAND
1961 26 Sept	Sir Seewoosagur Ramgoolam					
1963 1 Feb		Dr Hastings Banda *(Note 38)*				
1964 23 Jan			Kenneth Kaunda *(Note 38)*			
1965 3 Mar					Seretse Khama *(Note 38)*	
6 May				*Sekhonyana Maseribane		
7 July				Chief Leabua Jonathan		
1967 25 Apr						Prince Makhosini Dhlamini

		MAURITIUS	MALAWI	ZAMBIA	LESOTHO	BOTSWANA	SWAZILAND
1964	6 July			Kanyama Chiume			
	8 Sept			Dr Hastings Banda			
	24 Sept				Simon Kapwepwe		
1966	30 Sept						Sir Seretse Khama *(Note 67)*
	4 Oct					Chief Leabua Jonathan	
1967	7 Sept				Reuben Kamanga		
1968	12 Mar	Sir Seewoosagur Ramgoolam					
	6 Sept						Prince Makhosini Dlamini
	23 Dec				Elijah Mudenda		
1969	25 Aug				Kenneth Kaunda		
	1 Dec	Gaetan Duval					
1970	7 Oct				Elijah Mudenda		
1972	2 June						Stephen Matsebula
	July					Peete Peete	

MINISTERS OF DEFENCE

		MAURITIUS	MALAWI	ZAMBIA	LESOTHO	BOTSWANA	SWAZILAND
1964	23 Jan			Kenneth Kaunda			
	6 July		Dr Hastings Banda				
1966	4 Oct				Chief Leabua Jonathan		
1968	11 June	Sir Seewoosagur Ramgoolam					
1970	8 Jan			Alexander Grey Zulu			

	MAURITIUS	MALAWI	ZAMBIA	LESOTHO	BOTSWANA	SWAZILAND
1964 23 Jan			Simon Kapwepwe			
6 July		Yatuta Chisiza				
24 Sept			Mainza Chona			
Oct		Richard Chidzanja *(Note 68)*				
1965 11 May				Sekhonyana Maseribane		
1966 30 Sept					A M Dambe	
1967 1 Jan			Lewis Changufu			
24 Apr		Gwandanguluwe Chikanzi Chakuwamba				
7 Sept			Alexander Grey Zulu			
1 Nov		Gomile Kumtumanji				
1969 22 Oct					Moutlakgola Nwako	
24 Nov		Gladstone Ndaema				
1970 8 Jan			Lewis Changufu			
2 Mar				Chief Matete Majara		
24 Apr		Richard Sembereka				
1972 4 Apr		Pearson Makhumula Nkhoma				
2 June						Prince Masitsela
July				Gabriel Manyeli		
4 Sept		Malani Lungu				

	MAURITIUS	MALAWI	ZAMBIA	LESOTHO	BOTSWANA	SWAZILAND
1961 26 Sept	Sir Seewoosagur Ramgoolam					
1963 1 Feb		Henry Ellis Isidore Phillips				
1964 23 Jan			Arthur Wina			
6 July		John Tembo				
1965 11 May				Benedict Leseteli		
1966 30 Sept					Quett Ketumile Jonny Masire	
1967 16 May						Leo Lovell
8 July				Peete Peete		
15 Aug	Guy Forget					
7 Sept			Elijah Mudenda			
1968 12 Mar	Veeraswamy Ringadoo					
23 Dec			Simon Kapwepwe			
1969 1 Jan		Aleke Banda				
25 Aug			Elijah Mudenda			
22 Oct					James George Haskins	
1970 June					Quett Ketumile Jonny Masire	
2 Oct			John Mwanakatwe			
1971 31 Aug				R. E. Sekhonyana		
1972 4 Apr		Dick Matenje				
2 June						Robert Stephens

GOVERNORS/GOVERNORS-GENERAL/PRESIDENTS

	BAHAMAS	BARBADOS	BRITISH GUIANA	BRITISH HONDURAS	JAMAICA	TRINIDAD AND TOBAGO
1900 1 Jan	Sir Gilbert Carter	Sir James Shaw Hay	Sir Walter Sendall	Sir David Wilson	Sir Augustus Hemming	Sir Hubert Edward Jerningham
4 Dec						Sir Cornelius Alfred Moloney
1901 18 Feb		Sir Frederick Hodgson				
25 Dec			Sir Alexander Swettenham			
1904 15 Apr				Sir Bickham Sweet-Escott		
30 Aug						Sir Henry Moore Jackson
26 Sept			Sir Frederick Hodgson			
30 Sept					Sir Alexander Swettenham	
24 Oct		Sir Gilbert Carter				
29 Nov	Sir William Grey-Wilson					
1906 13 Aug				Sir Eric Swayne		
1907 16 May					Sir Sydney Olivier	
1909 12 May						Sir George Le Hunte
1911 13 Feb		Sir Leslie Probyn				
1912 5 July			Sir Walter Egerton			
29 Oct	Sir George Haddon-Smith					
1913 7 Mar					Sir William Manning	
19 May				Sir Wilfred Collett		
1915 15 June	Sir William Allardyce					
1916 1 June						Colonel Sir John Chancellor
1917 15 Apr			Sir Wilfred Collett			
1918 29 Jan				William Hart Bennett		
11 June					Sir Leslie Probyn	
27 Sept		Sir Charles O'Brien				
1919 22 Mar				Sir Eyre Hutson		

	BAHAMAS	BARBADOS	BRITISH GUIANA	BRITISH HONDURAS	JAMAICA	TRINIDAD AND TOBAGO
	Allardyce	O'Brien	Collett	Hutson	Probyn	Chancellor
1920 8 Dec	Sir Harry Cordeaux					
1922 1 Jan						Sir Samuel Wilson
1923 4 Apr			Sir Graeme Thomson			
29 Sept					Sir Samuel Wilson	
22 Nov						Sir Horace Byatt
1925 16 Apr				Sir John Burdon		
31 Aug			Sir Cecil Rodwell			
31 Dec		Sir William Robertson				
1926 26 Apr					Sir Reginald Stubbs	
1927 15 Mar	Sir Charles Orr					
1928 7 Nov			Brigadier-General Sir Gordon Guggisberg			
1930 22 Mar						Sir Alfred Claud Hollis
9 June			Sir Edward Denham			
1932 10 Jan	Sir Bede Clifford					
9 Mar				Sir Harold Kittermaster		
21 Nov					Sir Ransford Slater	
1933 Jan		Harry Scott Newlands				
5 Aug		Sir Mark Young				
1934 24 Oct					Sir Edward Denham	
2 Nov				Sir Alan Burns		
1935 26 Mar			Sir Geoffrey Northcote			
1936 17 Sept						Sir Murchison Fletcher
1937 19 Nov			Sir Wilfrid Jackson			
27 Nov	Sir Charles Dundas					
1938 8 July						Sir Mark Young

	BAHAMAS	BARBADOS	BRITISH GUIANA	BRITISH HONDURAS	JAMAICA	TRINIDAD AND TOBAGO
	Dundas	Young	Jackson	Burns	Denham	Young
1938 6 Aug		Sir Eubule John Waddington				
19 Aug					Sir Arthur Richards	
1940 24 Feb				Sir John Hunter		
18 Aug	H. R. H. the Duke of Windsor					
1941 23 Oct		Sir Grattan Bushe				
7 Nov			Sir Gordon Lethem			
1942 8 June						Sir Bede Clifford
1943 29 Sept					Sir John Huggins	
1945 28 July	Sir William Murphy					
1947 14 Jan				Sir Edward Gerald Hawkesworth		
5 Feb		Sir Hilary Blood				
7 Mar						Sir John Shaw
12 Apr			Sir Charles Woolley			
1949 28 Jan				Sir Ronald Garvey		
1 Nov		Sir Alfred Savage				
1950 5 Jan	Sir George Sandford					
19 Apr						General Sir Hubert Rance
7 Dec	General Sir Robert Neville					
1951 7 Apr					Sir Hugh Foot	
1952 21 Oct				Sir Patrick Renison		
1953 14 Apr			Sir Alfred Savage			
14 May		Sir Robert Arundell				
21 Dec	Earl of Ranfurly					
1955 23 June						Sir Edward Beetham
25 Oct			Sir Patrick Renison			

	BAHAMAS	BARBADOS	BRITISH GUIANA	BRITISH HONDURAS	JAMAICA	TRINIDAD AND TOBAGO
	Ranfurly	Arundell	Renison	Renison	Foot	Beetham
1956 17 Jan				Sir Colin Thornley		
1957 1 Apr	Sir Raynor Arthur					
18 Dec					Sir Kenneth Blackburne *(Note 69)*	
1959 8 Oct		Sir John Stow				
22 Dec			Sir Ralph Grey			
1960 14 July						Sir Solomon Hochoy *(Note 70)*
18 July	Sir Robert Stapledon					
1961 9 Dec				Sir Peter Stallard		
1962 1 Dec					Sir Clifford Campbell	
1964 7 Mar			Sir Richard Luyt			
3 June	Sir Ralph Grey					
1966 11 July				Sir John Paul		
16 Dec			Sir David James Gardiner Rose			
1967 15 May		Sir Arleigh Winston Scott				
1968 Oct	Sir Francis Cumming-Bruce, Lord Thurlow					
1970 17 Mar			Arthur Chung *(Note 46)*			
1972 Jan				Richard Posnett		
14 Apr	Sir John Paul					

	BAHAMAS	BARBADOS	BRITISH GUIANA	BRITISH HONDURAS	JAMAICA	TRINIDAD AND TOBAGO
1953 5 May					Sir Alexander Bustamente	
30 May			Dr Cheddi Jagan			
9 Oct			*Constitution suspended*			
1954 1 Feb		Sir Grantley Adams				
1955 2 Feb					Norman Manley	
1956 28 Oct						Dr Eric Williams
1958 10 Apr		Dr Gordon Cummins *(Note 71)*				
1961 7 Apr				George Cadle Price		
5 Sept			Dr Cheddi Jagan			
8 Dec		Errol Walter Barrow				
1962 11 Apr					Sir Alexander Bustamente	
1964 7 Jan	Sir Roland Theodore Symonette					
12 Dec			Forbes Burnham			
1967 16 Jan	Lynden Oscar Pindling					
22 Feb					Sir Donald Sangster	
11 Apr					Hugh Lawson Shearer	
1972 2 Mar					Michael Manley	

MINISTERS OF FOREIGN AFFAIRS

	BAHAMAS	BARBADOS	GUYANA	BRITISH HONDURAS	JAMAICA	TRINIDAD AND TOBAGO
1961 19 Dec						Dr Eric Williams
1962 6 Aug					Sir Alexander Bustamente	
1966 15 Jan			Forbes Burnham *(Note 72)*			
30 Nov		Errol Walter Barrow				
1967 2 Mar					Hugh Lawson Shearer	
5 Apr						Arthur Napoleon Raymond Robinson
1970 14 Apr						Dr Eric Williams
3 July						Francis Casimir Prevatt
1971 27 May						Kamaluddin Mohammed
1972 10 Mar					Michael Manley	
1 Aug			Shridath Surendranath Ramphal			

MINISTERS OF THE INTERIOR

	BAHAMAS	BARBADOS	GUYANA	BRITISH HONDURAS	JAMAICA	TRINIDAD AND TOBAGO
1957 11 Nov					Dr Ivan Lloyd	
1959 20 July						Patrick Joseph Solomon
15 Aug					William McKenzie Seivright	
1961 5 Sept			Balram Singh Rai			
1962 11 Apr					Roy Ambrose McNeil	
18 June			Claude Christian			
1963 17 June			Mrs Janet Jagan			
1964 1 Jan				Carl Lindberg Bernard Rogers		
3 June			Brindley Horatio Benn			
16 Sept						Albert Gerard Montano
21 Dec			Dr Ptolemy Alexander Reid			
1966 28 Nov		Philip Marlowe Greaves				
1967 26 Jan	Jeffrey McDonald Reid					
31 Dec			Clifton Mortimer Llewellyn John			
1969 7 Jan			Dr Ptolemy Alexander Reid			
Jan	Arthur Dion Hanna					
18 Feb			Hugh Desmond Hoyte			
1970 29 June						Dr Eric Williams
31 Dec			Oscar Clarke			
1971 27 May						Albert Gerard Montano
1972 10 Mar					Noel Percival Silvera	

MINISTERS OF FINANCE

		BAHAMAS	BARBADOS	BRITISH GUIANA	BRITISH HONDURAS	JAMAICA	TRINIDAD AND TOBAGO
1953	5 May					Donald Sangster	
1954	1 Feb		Sir Grantley Adams				
1955	4 Feb					Norman Newton Nethersole	
1956	28 Oct						Dr Eric Williams
1958	10 Apr		Dr Gordon Cummins				
1959	30 May					Vernon Leonard Arnett	
1961	7 Apr				George Cadle Price		
	5 Sept			Charles Jacob			
	8 Dec		Errol Walter Barrow				
	19 Dec						Arthur Napoleon Raymond Robinson
1962	11 Apr					Donald Sangster	
1964	7 Jan	Sir Stafford Sands					
	21 Dec			Peter Stanislaus D'Aguiar			
1967	26 Jan	Carleton Elisha Francis					
	28 Mar					Edward Philip George Seaga	
	5 Apr						Dr Eric Williams
	25 Sept			Dr Ptolemy Alexander Reid			
1970	31 Dec			Hugh Desmond Hoyte			
1971	27 May						George Michael Chambers
1972	10 Mar					David Coore	
	1 Aug			Frank Hope			

		TONGA RULER	TONGA PREMIER	HIGH COMMIS- SIONER FOR THE WESTERN PACIFIC	FIJI GOVERNOR	FIJI PREMIER	NAURU PRESIDENT	WESTERN SAMOA HEAD OF STATE	PREMIER
1900	1 Jan	George II	Jiosateki Toga	Sir George O'Brien	Until 1952 the High Commissioner was also Governor of Fiji				
1902	10 Sept			Sir Henry Jackson					
1904	11 Oct			Sir Everard im Thurn					
1905	Jan		Jione Mateialona						
1911	21 Feb			Sir Henry May					
1912	25 July			Sir Bickham Sweet- Escott					
	30 Sept		Tevita Tuivakano						
1918	5 Apr	Salote							
	10 Oct			Sir Cecil Rodwell					
1922	30 June		Prince Consort Uiliami Tugi						
1925	25 Apr			Sir Eyre Hutson					
1929	22 Nov			Sir Murchison Fletcher					
1936	28 Nov			Sir Arthur Richards					
1938	16 Sept			Sir Harry Luke					
1940	July		Ata						
1942	21 July			Sir Philip Mitchell					
1945	1 Jan			Sir Alexander Grantham					
1948	20 Jan			Sir Brian Freeston					
1949	12 Dec		Crown Prince Taufa'ahua Tungi						
1952	3 July			Sir Robert Stanley					
	6 Oct				Sir Ronald Garvey				
1955	26 Sept			Sir John Gutch					
1958	28 Oct				Sir Kenneth Maddocks				
1961	4 Mar			Sir David Trench					

		TONGA RULER	TONGA PREMIER	HIGH COMMISSIONER FOR THE WESTERN PACIFIC	FIJI GOVERNORS	FIJI PREMIER	NAURU PRESIDENT	WESTERN SAMOA HEAD OF STATE	PREMIER
1962	1 Jan	Salote	Tungi	Trench	Maddocks			Tupua Tamase Mea'ole *and (Note 73)* Malietoa Tanumafili II	Fiame II Mata'afa Faumuina Mulinu'u
1964	8 Jan				Sir Derek Jakeway				
	16 June			Sir Robert Foster					
1965	16 Dec	Taufa'ahua	Prince Tu'ipelehake						
1967	1 Sept					Ratu Sir Kamisese Mara			
1968	31 Jan						Hammer DeRoburt		
	Dec				Sir Robert Foster				
1969	6 Mar			Sir Michael Gass					
1970	Feb							Tupua Tamasese Leolofi IV	

PREMIERS OF THE EASTERN CANADIAN PROVINCES

		NEW-FOUNDLAND	PRINCE EDWARD ISLAND	NOVA SCOTIA	NEW BRUNSWICK	QUEBEC
1900	1 Jan		Donald Farquharson	George Henry Murray	Henry Robert Emmerson	Félix Gabriel Marchand
	31 Aug				Lemuel John Tweedie	
	3 Oct					Simon Napoléon Parent
1901	29 Dec		Arthur Peters			
1905	23 Mar					Sir Jean Lomer Gouin
1907	6 Mar				William Pugsley	
	31 May				Christopher William Robinson	
1908	1 Feb		Francis Longworth Haszard			
	24 Mar				John Douglas Hazen	
1911	16 May		Herbert James Palmer			
	16 Oct				James Kidd Fleming	
	2 Dec		John Alexander Mathieson			
1914	17 Dec				George Johnson Clarke	
1917	1 Feb				James Murray	
	4 Apr				Walter Edward Foster	
	21 June		Aubin Arsenault			
1919	9 Sept		John Howatt Bell			
1920	8 July					Louis Alexandre Taschereau
1923	24 Jan			Ernest Howard Armstrong		
	28 Feb				Peter John Veniot	
	5 Sept		James Stewart			

	NEW-FOUNDLAND	PRINCE EDWARD ISLAND	NOVA SCOTIA	NEW BRUNSWICK	QUEBEC
		Stewart	Armstrong	Veniot	Taschereau
1925 16 July			Edgar Nelson Rhodes		
14 Sept				John Babington Macaulay Baxter	
1927 12 Aug		Albert Charles Saunders			
1930 20 May		Walter Maxfield Lea			
11 Aug			Gordon Sidney Harrington		
1931 19 May				Charles Dow Richards	
29 Aug		James Stewart			
1933 1 June				Leonard Percy de Wolfe Tilley	
5 Sept			Angus Lewis Macdonald		
14 Oct		William MacMillan			
1935 16 July				Allison Dysart	
15 Aug		Walter Maxfield Lea			
1936 14 Jan		Thane Campbell			
11 June					Joseph Adélard Godbout
26 Aug					Maurice Duplessis
1939 9 Nov					Joseph Adélard Godbout
1940 13 Mar				John Babbitt McNair	
10 July			Alexander Stirling MacMillan		
1943 11 May		John Walter Jones			
1944 30 Aug					Maurice Duplessis

		NEW-FOUNDLAND	PRINCE EDWARD ISLAND	NOVA SCOTIA	NEW BRUNSWICK	QUEBEC
			Jones	MacMillan	McNair	Duplessis
1945	8 Sept			Angus Lewis Macdonald		
1949	1 Apr	Joseph Smallwood				
1952	8 Oct				Hugh John Flemming	
1953	25 May		Alexander Mathieson			
1954	13 Apr			Harold Connolly		
	30 Sept			Henry Davies Hicks		
1956	20 Nov			Robert Stanfield		
1959	11 Sept					Joseph Paul Sauvé
	16 Sept		Walter Shaw			
1960	8 Jan					Antonio Barrette
	12 July				Louis Robichaud	
	22 July					Jean Lesage
1966	5 June					Daniel Johnson
	28 July		Alexander Bradshaw Campbell			
1967	13 Sept			George Isaac Smith		
1968	2 Oct					Jean Jacques Bertrand
1970	29 Apr					Robert Bourassa
	28 Oct			Gerald Augustine Regan		
	12 Nov				Richard Bennett Hatfield	
1972	18 Jan	Frank Duff Moores				

PREMIERS OF THE CENTRAL AND WESTERN CANADIAN PROVINCES

		ONTARIO	MANITOBA	SASKATCH-EWAN	ALBERTA	BRITISH COLUMBIA
1900	1 Jan	George William Ross	Thomas Greenway			Charles Augustus Semlin
	6 Jan		Hugh John Macdonald			
	28 Feb					Joseph Martin
	14 June					James Dunsmuir
	29 Oct		Sir Rodmond Palen Roblin			
1902	21 Nov					Edward Gawler Prior
1903	6 June					Sir Richard McBride
1905	8 Feb	Sir James Pliny Whitney				
	2 Sept				Alexander Rutherford	
	5 Sept			Walter Scott		
1910	26 May				Arthur Lewis Sifton	
1914	2 Oct	Sir William Howard Hearst				
1915	12 May		Tobias Crawford Norris			
	15 Dec					William John Bowser
1916	23 Nov					Harlan Carey Brewster
	20 Oct			William Martin		
1917	30 Oct				Charles Stewart	
1918	6 Mar					John Oliver
1919	14 Nov	Ernest Charles Drury				
1921	13 Aug				Herbert Greenfield	
1922	5 Apr			Charles Avery Dunning		
	8 Aug		John Bracken			
1923	16 July	George Howard Ferguson				

		ONTARIO	MANITOBA	SASKATCH-EWAN	ALBERTA	BRITISH COLUMBIA
		Ferguson	Bracken	Dunning	Greenfield	Oliver
1925	23 Nov				John Edward Brownlee	
1926	26 Feb			James Gardiner		
1927	20 Aug					John Duncan MacLean
1928	21 Aug					Simon Fraser Tolmie
1929	9 Sept			James Thomas Milton Anderson		
1930	15 Dec	George Stewart Henry				
1933	15 Nov					Thomas Dufferin Pattullo
1934	10 July	Mitchell Frederick Hepburn			Richard Gavin Reid	
	19 July			James Gardiner		
1935	3 Sept				William Aberhart	
	1 Nov			William Patterson		
1941	10 Dec					John Hart
1942	21 Oct	Gordon Daniel Conant				
1943	8 Jan		Stuart Sinclair Garson			
	18 May	Harry Corwin Nixon				
	31 May				Ernest Manning	
	17 Aug	George Alexander Drew				
1944	10 July			Thomas Clement Douglas		
1947	29 Dec					Byron Johnson
1948	19 Oct	Thomas Laird Kennedy				
	7 Nov		Douglas Lloyd Campbell			

		ONTARIO	MANITOBA	SASKATCH-EWAN	ALBERTA	BRITISH COLUMBIA
		Kennedy	Campbell	Douglas	Manning	Johnson
1949	4 May	Leslie Frost				
1952	1 Aug					William Andrew Cecil Bennett
1958	16 June		Dufferin Roblin			
1961	7 Nov			Woodrow Stanley Lloyd		
	8 Nov	John Robarts				
1964	22 May			Wilbert Ross Thatcher		
1967	25 Nov		Walter Weir			
1968	12 Dec				Harry Strom	
1969	15 July		Edward Schreyer			
1971	1 Mar	William Grenville Davis				
	30 June			Allan Emrys Blakeney		
	10 Sept				Peter Lougheed	
1972	31 Aug					David Barrett

PREMIERS OF AUSTRALIAN STATES

		NEW SOUTH WALES	QUEENSLAND	SOUTH AUSTRALIA	TASMANIA	VICTORIA	WESTERN AUSTRALIA
1900	1 Jan	Sir William John Lyne	Robert Philp	Frederick William Holder	Sir Neil Elliot Lewis	Allan McLean	Sir John Forrest
	19 Nov					Sir George Turner	
1901	12 Feb					Sir Alexander James Peacock	
	15 Feb						George Throssell
	28 Mar	Sir John See					
	15 May			John Greeley Jenkins			
	27 May						George Leake
	21 Nov						Alfred Edward Morgans
	23 Dec						George Leake
1902	10 June					William Hill Irvine	
	1 July						Walter James
1903	9 Apr				William Bisphen Propsting		
	17 Sept		Arthur Morgan				
1904	16 Feb					Sir Thomas Bent	
	15 June	Thomas Waddell					
	10 Aug						Henry Daglish
	30 Aug	Joseph Hector Carruthers					
1905	1 Mar			Richard Butler			
	26 July			Thomas Price			
	25 Aug						Cornthwaite Hector Rason
1906	19 Jan		William Kidston				
	7 May						Newton James Moore
1907	11 July				John William Evans		
	2 Oct	Charles Gregory Wade					

		NEW SOUTH WALES	QUEENSLAND	SOUTH AUSTRALIA	TASMANIA	VICTORIA	WESTERN AUSTRALIA
		Wade	Kidston	Price	Evans	Bent	Moore
1907	19 Nov		Robert Philp				
1908	18 Feb		William Kidston				
1909	8 Jan					John Murray	
	5 June			Archibald Peake			
	19 June				Sir Neil Elliot Lewis		
	20 Oct				John Earle		
	27 Oct				Sir Neil Elliot Lewis		
1910	3 June			John Verran			
	16 Sept						Frank Wilson
	21 Oct	James Sinclair Taylor McGowen					
1911	7 Feb		Digby Frank Denham				
	7 Oct						John Scaddan
1912	17 Feb			Archibald Peake			
	18 May					William Alexander Watt	
	14 June				Albert Edgar Solomon		
1913	30 June	William Holman					
	9 Dec					George Alexander Elmslie	
	22 Dec					William Alexander Watt	
1914	6 Apr				John Earle		
	18 June					Sir Alexander James Peacock	
1915	3 Apr			Crawford Vaughan			

	NEW SOUTH WALES	QUEENSLAND	SOUTH AUSTRALIA	TASMANIA	VICTORIA	WESTERN AUSTRALIA
	Holman	Denham	Vaughan	Earle	Peacock	Scaddan
1915 1 June		Thomas Joseph Ryan				
1916 15 Apr				Sir Walter Lee		
27 July						Frank Wilson
1917 28 June						Sir Henry Bruce Lefroy
14 July			Archibald Peake			
29 Nov					John Bowser	
1918 21 Mar					Harry Sutherland Wightman Lawson	
1919 17 Apr						Sir Hal Colebatch
17 May						James Mitchell
22 Oct		Edward Granville Theodore				
1920 8 Apr			Sir Henry Barwell			
13 Apr	John Storey					
1921 10 Oct	James Dooley					
20 Dec	Sir George Fuller					
20 Dec	James Dooley					
1922 13 Apr	Sir George Fuller					
12 Aug				John Blyth Hayes		
1923 14 Aug				Sir Walter Lee		
25 Oct				Joseph Aloysius Lyons		
1924 16 Apr			John Gunn			Philip Collier
28 Apr					Sir Alexander James Peacock	
18 July					George Michael Prendergast	
18 Nov					John Allan	

(AUS)

	NEW SOUTH WALES	QUEENSLAND	SOUTH AUSTRALIA	TASMANIA	VICTORIA	WESTERN AUSTRALIA
	Fuller	Theodore	Gunn	Lyons	Allan	Collier
1925 25 Feb		William Neal Gillies				
17 June	John Lang					
22 Oct		William McCormack				
1926 28 Aug			Lionel Hill			
1927 8 Apr			Richard Layton Butler			
20 May					Edmond John Hogan	
19 Oct	Thomas Rainsford Bavin					
1928 15 June				John Cameron McPhee		
22 Nov					Sir William Murray McPherson	
1929 21 May		Arthur Moore				
12 Dec					Edmond John Hogan	
1930 17 Apr			Lionel Hill			
24 Apr						Sir James Mitchell
4 Nov	John Lang					
1932 13 May	Bertram Stevens					
19 May					Sir Stanley Seymour Argyle	
17 June		William Forgan Smith				
1933 13 Feb			Robert Stanley Richards			
18 Apr			Richard Layton Butler			
24 Apr						Philip Collier
1934 15 Mar				Sir Walter Lee		
22 June				Albert George Ogilvie		

		NEW SOUTH WALES	QUEENSLAND	SOUTH AUSTRALIA	TASMANIA	VICTORIA	WESTERN AUSTRALIA
		Stevens	Smith	Butler	Ogilvie	Argyle	Collier
1935	2 Apr					Albert Arthur Dunstan	
1936	20 Aug						John Collings Willcock
1938	5 Nov			Sir Thomas Playford			
1939	11 June				Edmund Dwyer-Gray		
	5 Aug	Alexander Mair					
	18 Dec				Robert Cosgrove		
1941	16 May	William John McKell					
1942	16 Sept		Frank Arthur Cooper				
1943	14 Sept					John Cain	
	18 Sept					Albert Arthur Dunstan	
1945	31 July						Frank Joseph Scott Wise
	2 Oct					Ian MacFarlan	
	21 Nov					John Cain	
1946	7 Mar		Edward Michael Hanlon				
1947	6 Feb	James McGirr					
	1 Apr						Duncan Ross McLarty
	20 Nov					Thomas Tuke Hollway	
	18 Dec				Edward Brooker		
1948	25 Feb				Robert Cosgrove		
1950	27 June					John Gladstone Black McDonald	
1952	17 Jan		Vincent Clair Gare				

		NEW SOUTH WALES	QUEENSLAND	SOUTH AUSTRALIA	TASMANIA	VICTORIA	WESTERN AUSTRALIA
		McGirr	Gare	Playford	Cosgrove	McDonald	McLarty
1952	2 Apr	John Joseph Cahill					
	28 Oct					Thomas Tuke Hollway	
	31 Oct					John Gladstone Black McDonald	
	17 Dec					John Cain	
1953	23 Feb						Albert Redvers George Hawke
1955	7 June					Sir Henry Edward Bolte	
1957	12 Aug		Francis Nicklin				
1958	26 Aug				Eric Elliot Reece		
1959	2 Apr						Sir David Brand
	23 Oct	Robert James Heffron					
1964	30 Apr	John Brophy Renshaw					
1965	10 Mar			Frank Walsh			
	13 May	Robert William Askin					
1967	1 June			Donald Allen Dunstan			
1968	17 Jan		John Charles Allan Pizzey				
	17 Apr			Raymond Steele Hall			
	1 Aug		Gordon William Chalk				
	8 Aug		Johannes Bjelke-Petersen				
1969	26 May				Walter Angus Bethune		

		NEW SOUTH WALES	QUEENSLAND	SOUTH AUSTRALIA	TASMANIA	VICTORIA	WESTERN AUSTRALIA
		Askin	Petersen	Hall	Bethune	Bolte	Brand
1970	2 June			Donald Allan Dunstan			
1971	3 Mar						John Tresize Tonkin
1972	3 May				Eric Elliot Reece		
	22 Aug					Rupert James Hamer	

	ANDHRA PRADESH	ASSAM	BIHAR	GUJARAT	HARYANA	HIMACHAL PRADESH	KASHMIR
1946 1 Feb		Gopinath Bardoloi					
23 Mar			Srikrishna Sinha				
1948 17 Mar							Sheikh Abdillah
1950 Aug		Bishnuram Medhi					
1953 9 Aug							Bakshi Ghulam Mohammed
6 Oct	T Prakasam						
1954 15 Nov	*Governor's rule*						
1955 28 Mar	B. Gopala Reddy						
1956 1 Nov	Neelam Sanjiva Reddy						
1957 28 Dec		Bimali Prasad Chaliha					
1960 11 Jan	Damodaram Sanjiviah						
1 May				Dr Jivraj Mehta			
1961 8 Feb			Pandit Binodanand Jha				
1962 12 Mar	Neelam Sanjivah Reddy						
1963 18 Sept				Balwantrai Mehta			
2 Oct			Krishna Ballabh Sahay				
12 Oct							Khwaja Shamsuddin
1964 28 Feb							Ghulam Mohammed Sadiq
29 Feb	Brahmananda Reddy						
1965 20 Sept				Hitendra Kanaiyalal Desai			
1966 1 Nov					Bhagwat Dayal Sharma		
1967 5 Mar			Mahamaya Prasad Sinha				
24 Mar					Rao Birendra Singh		
21 Nov					*Presidential rule*		

	ANDHRA PRADESH	ASSAM	BIHAR	GUJARAT	HARYANA	HIMACHAL PRADESH	KASHMIR
	Reddy	Chaliha	Sinha	Desai	*Presidential rule*		Sadiq
1968 1 Feb			B. P. Mandal				
22 Mar			Bhola Paswan Shastri				
21 May					Bansi Lal		
29 June			*Presidential rule*				
1969 26 Feb			Harihar Prasad Singh				
22 June			Bhola Paswan Shastri				
4 July			*Presidential rule*				
1970 16 Feb			Daroga Prasad Rai				
6 Nov		Mahendra Mohan Choudhury					
22 Dec			Karpoori Thakur				
1971 25 Jan						Dr Y.S. Parmar	
13 May				*Presidential Rule*			
2 June			Bhola Paswan Shastri				
30 Sept	V. P. Narasinha Rao						
12 Dec							Syed Mir Qasim
1972 9 Jan			*Presidential rule*				
31 Jan		Sarat Chandra Sinha					
17 Mar				Ghanshyam Oza			
19 Mar			Kedar Pandey				

	KERALA (TRAVAN-CORE-COCHIN)	MADHYA PRADESH (CENTRAL PROVINCES)	MAHARASH-TRA (BOMBAY)	MANIPUR	MEGHALAYA	MYSORE	NAGALAND
	(Note 74)						
1946 30 Mar			B.G. Kher				
20 Apr		Pandit Ravishankar Shukla					
1947 24 Oct						K.C. Reddy	
1948 24 Mar	Pattom Thanu Pillai						
20 Oct	T.K. Narayana Pillai						
1952 Jan	C Kesavan						
12 Mar	A.J. John						
21 Apr			Morarji Desai				
1954 16 Mar	Pattom Thanu Pillai						
4 Apr						K Hanumathaiya	
1955 10 Feb	Panamapilli Govinda Menon						
1956 23 Mar	*Presidential rule*						
19 Aug	*None*					Kadiwal Manjappa	
1 Nov			Yeshwantrao Balwantrao Chavan *(Note 75)*			Siddavvanahalli Nijalingappa	
1957 31 Jan		Dr Kailas Nath Katju					
5 Apr	E.M. Nambooridapad						
1958 16 May						B.D. Jatti	
1959 31 July	*Presidential rule*						
1960 22 Feb	Pattom Thanu Pillai						
1962 8 Mar						S.R. Kanthi	
11 Mar		Bhagwantarai Mandloi					
21 Jun						Siddavvanahalli Nijalingappa	
25 Sept	R Sankar						

	KERALA (TRAVAN-CORE-COCHIN)	MADHYA PRADESH (CENTRAL PROVINCES)	MAHARASHTRA (BOMBAY)	MANIPUR	MEGHALAYA	MYSORE	NAGALAND
	Sankar	Mandloi	Chavan (Note 75)			Nijalingappa	
1962 19 Nov			Marotrao Sambashio Kannamwar				
1963 30 Sept		Dr Dwarka Prasad Mishra					
1 Dec			V.P. Naik				Shilu Ao
1964 10 Sept	*Presidential rule*						
1966 14 Aug							T.N. Angami
1967 5 Mar	E.M. Nambooridapad						
30 July		Govind Narain Singh					
1968 29 May						Veerendra Patil	
1969 22 Feb							Hokishe Sema
13 Mar		Raja Naresh Chandra Singh					
26 Mar		Shyama Charam Shukla					
1 Nov	C. Acutha Menon						
1970 4 Aug	*Presidential rule*						
4 Oct	C. Acutha Menon						
1971 27 Mar						*Presidential rule*	
1972 20 Jan					Captain Williamson Sangma		
21 Jan				*Presidential rule*			
29 Jan		Prakash Chandra Sethi					
20 Mar				Mohammed Alimuddin		Devaraj Urs	

	ORISSA	PUNJAB	RAJASTHAN	TAMIL NADU (MADRAS)	TRIPURA	UTTAR PRADESH (UNITED PROVINCES)	WEST BENGAL
1946 1 Apr				*(Note 76)*		Pandit Govin Pant	
23 Apr	Harekrushna Mahatab						
30 Apr				T Prakasam			
1947 23 Mar				Amandur Ramaswami Reddiar			
3 July							P.C. Ghosh
Aug		Dr Gopichand Bhargava					
1948 14 Jan							Dr Bidhai Chandra Roy
25 Mar			Manik Lal Vermu				
1949 6 Apr				O. P. Kumaraswami Raja			
21 Apr		Bhimsen Sachar					
17 Oct		Dr Gopichand Bhargava					
1950 12 May	Nabakrishna Choudhuri						
1951 26 Apr			Jainarain Vyas				
20 June			*Presidential rule*				
1952 10 Apr				Chakravarti Rajagopalachari			
17 Apr		Bhimsen Sachar					
1954 13 Apr				K. Kamaraj (Nadar)			
13 Nov			Mohanlal Sukhadia				
18 Dec						Dr Sampurnanand	
1956 15 Jan		Sardar Pratrap Singh Kairon					
15 Oct	Harekrushna Mahatab						
1960 1 Dec						Chandra Bhanu Gupta	
1961 16 June	Bijayananda Patnaik						
1962 8 July							Prafulla Chandra Sen

	ORISSA	PUNJAB	RAJASTHAN	TAMIL NADU (MADRAS)	TRIPURA	UTTAR PRADESH (UNITED PROVINCES)	WEST BENGAL
	Patnaik	Kairon	Sukhadia	Kamaraj		Gupta	Sen
1963 2 Oct	Biren Mitra			M Bhaktavsalam		Mrs Sucheta Kripalani	
1964 21 June		*Dr Gopichand Bhargava					
6 July		Ram Kishan					
1965 21 Feb	Sadasiba Tripathi						
1966 1 Nov		Gurmukh Singh Musafir					
1967 4 Mar				Conjeeveram Natarajna Annadurai			
5 Mar							Akoy Mukerjee
8 Mar	R. N. Singh Deo	Sardar Gurinam Singh					
13 Mar			*Presidential rule*				
14 Mar						Chandra Bhanu Gupta	
3 Apr						Charan Singh	
26 Apr			Mohanlal Sukhadia				
21 Nov							P. C. Ghosh
27 Nov		Lachman Singh Gill					
1968 20 Feb							*Presidential rule*
15 Apr						*Presidential rule*	
23 Aug		*Presidential rule*					
1969 10 Feb				Muthuvel Karunanidhi			
17 Feb		Sardar Gurinam Singh					
25 Feb						Chandra Bhanu Gupta	Akoy Mukerjee
1970 17 Feb						Charan Singh	
19 Mar							*Presidential rule*
27 Mar		Prakash Singh Badal					
2 Oct						*Presidential rule*	

	ORISSA	PUNJAB	RAJASTHAN	TAMIL NADU (MADRAS)	TRIPURA	UTTAR PRADESH (UNITED PROVINCES)	WEST BENGAL
	Singh Deo	Badal	Sukhadia	Karunanidhi		*Presidential rule*	*Presidential rule*
1970 18 Oct						Tribhuvan Narayan Singh	
1971 11 Jan	*Presidential rule*						
2 Apr							Akoy Mukerjee
3 Apr	Biswanath Das						
4 Apr						Kamlapati Tripathi	
15 June		*Presidential rule*					
28 June							*Presidential Rule*
8 July			Barkatullah Khan				
1972 21 Jan					*Presidential rule*		
17 Mar		Giani Zall Singh					
20 Mar							S. S. Ray
27 Mar					Sukhamoy Sengupta		
13 June	Mrs Nandini Satpathy						

| | | ANTIGUA | LEEWARD ISLANDS | | WINDWARD ISLANDS | | | ST VINCENT |
			MONTSER-RAT	ST KITTS	DOMINICA	GRENADA	ST LUCIA	
1960	1 Jan	Vere Cornwall Bird	William Henry Bramble	C. Paul Southwell	Franklin Arthur Merrifield Baron	Herbert Augustus Blaize	George Charles	Ebenezer Theodore Joshua
1961	Jan				Edward Oliver Le Blanc			
	Mar					George Clyne		
	Aug					Eric Gairy		
1962	19 June					*Constitution suspended*		
	Sept					Herbert Augustus Blaize		
1964	Apr						John Compton	
1966	July			Robert Bradshaw				
1967	May							Robert Milton Cato
	Aug					Eric Gairy		
1970	Feb	George Walter						
	Dec		Percival Austin Bramble					

	SELANGOR	PERAK	NEGRI SEMBILAN	PAHANG
1900 1 Jan	Alaidin Suleiman Shah	Sir Idris ibn Iskander	Sir Muham- mad ibn Antah	Ahmad Maatham Shah
1914 29 May				Mahmud ibn Ahmad
1916 17 Jan		Abduljalil ibn Rahmatullah		
1917 19 June				Abdullah ibn Ahmad
1918 26 Oct		Sir Iskander Shah		
1932 23 June				Sir Abu Bakar Ri'ayat ul-Din
1933 3 Aug			Sir Abdul Rahman ibn Muhammad	
1938 4 Apr	Sir Hisamuddin Alam Shah			
Oct		Abdul-Aziz al-Mutassim Billah		
1948 31 Mar		Sir Yussuf Izzudin Shah		
1957 31 Aug			Munawir ibn Abdul Rahman	
1960 3 Sept	Salahuddin Abdul-Aziz ibn Hisamuddin			
1963 6 Jan		Idris ibn Iskander		
1968 18 Apr			Jafar ibn Abdul Rahman	

RULERS OF OTHER MALAY STATES

	JOHORE	KEDAH	KELENTAN	PERLIS	TRENGGANU	BRUNEI	SARAWAK
1900 1 Jan	Sir Ibrahim ibn Abu Bakar	Abdulhamid ibn Halimshah	Long Snik ibn Muhammad		Zainal Abdin	Hassim Jalalulam	Sir Charles Johnson Brooke
1905 22 Dec				Syed Alawi ibn Safi			
1906 May						Sir Mohammed Jamalulam	
1914			Muhammad IV				
1917 17 May							Sir Charles Vyner Brooke
1918 25 Nov					Muhammad ibn Zainal Abdin		
1920 26 May					Sir Suleiman ibn Zainal Abdin		
20 Dec			Sir Ismail ibn Muhammad IV				
1924 Sept						Sir Ahmad Tajudin	
1941 16 Dec							*Overrun by Japanese forces*
1943 15 May		Sir Badlishah ibn Abdulhamid					
1944 21 June			Sir Ibrahim ibn Muhammad IV				
1945 4 Dec				Sir Putra ibn Hassan Jamulullah			
16 Dec					Sir Ismail Nasiruddin Shah		
1946 1 July							*Ceded to the Crown*
1950 6 June						Sir Omar Ali Saifuddin	
1958 14 July		Abdulhalim ibn Badlishah					
1959 8 May	Sir Ismail ibn Ibrahim						
1960 10 July			Yahya ibn Ibrahim				
1967 5 Oct						Sir Hassanal Bolkiah	

Notes

1. From June 1917 he and his successors had the title of Governor-General.

2. Sir John Kennedy and his two immediate successors were Governors of Southern Rhodesia. From 1953 to December 1963 there were also Governors-General of the Federation of Rhodesia and Nyasaland. These were Lord Llewellin (appointed 4 September 1953) and Lord Dalhousie (appointed 24 April 1957). Sir Humphrey Gibbs acted as Governor-General in the summer of 1963.

3. Sir Humphrey Gibbs remained nominally Governor of Rhodesia until 24 June 1969. In practice the Government of Ian Smith ignored him after the declaration of U.D.I. in November 1965.

4. Swart assumed office as President of the Republic of South Africa on 31 May 1961. He had previously been Governor-General.

5. Dupont was appointed Officer Administering the Government after U.D.I. He became President in March 1970.

6. Dr Theophilus Ebenaeser Dönges was elected President but was too ill to assume office. Naudé acted until there was a new election.

7. When the Federation of Rhodesia was established Huggins became its Prime Minister. He assumed office on 7 September 1953 and was succeeded by Sir Roy Welensky on 1 November 1956. He remained in office until the dissolution of the Federation in December 1963.

8. The Canadians listed until 1920 are Secretaries of State. They sometimes seem to have had the additional office of Minister for External Affairs and at other times the latter post does not seem to have been filled.

9. The Portfolio of External Affairs of the Federation was always held by the Prime Minister. Therefore it was Sir Godfrey Huggins (7 September 1953 to 1 November 1956) and Sir Roy Welensky (1 November 1956 to 31 December 1963).

10. During the First World War the Canadians had two Ministers of War, one of whom was stationed in Europe. Sir Albert Kemp served in the post abroad until 1920.

11. After the outbreak of the Second World War, the Prime Minister, Menzies, assumed responsibility for the Co-ordination of Defence.

12. The Prime Minister, Curtin, was Minister for Defence until 15 August 1946.

13. This and subsequent names are those of Ministers of Defence. The Secretary of State for War ceased to be a member of the Cabinet.

14. The Ministers of Defence of the Federation of Rhodesia and Nyasaland were Sir Godfrey Huggins (7 September 1953 to 1 November 1956), Sir Roy Welensky (1 November 1956 to 4 June 1959), John Caldicott (4 June 1959 to 3 May 1962) and Sir Malcolm Barrow (3 May 1962 to 31 December 1963).

15. Leggate was the first Minister of the Interior. Before July 1933 he and his predecessors were entitled Colonial Secretary.

16. Since this appointment I have not found a Minister of the Interior in any Canadian Cabinet list.

17. Lord Addison and his successors bore the title of Secretary of State for Commonwealth Relations from 2 July 1947.

18. The Ministers of the Interior of the Federation of Rhodesia and Nyasaland were Julian Greenfield (28 January 1954 to 7 January 1955), Frank Stephen Owen (7 January 1955 to 1 November 1956), Sir Malcolm Barrow (1 November 1956 to 3 May 1962) and Julian Greenfield again (3 May 1962 to 31 December 1963).

19. From 1942 to 1944 Walter Nash was Minister in Washington while still nominally Minister of Finance. The Prime Minister, Fraser, acted as Minister of Finance.

20. The Ministers of Finance of the Federation of Rhodesia and Nyasaland were Sir Donald McIntyre (17 December 1953 to 3 September 1962) and Sir John Caldicott (3 September 1962 to 31 December 1963).

21. Lord Ampthill acted as Viceroy from 20 April to 13 December 1904.

22. Monck-Mason Moore became Governor-General on 4 February 1948.

23. Lord Mountbatten became Governor-General of India after partition.

24. Lord Listowel ceased to be Secretary of State for India on 15 August 1947. He remained Secretary of State for Burma until 4 January 1948.

25. MacDonald and Scott were Governors-General and High Commissioners for South East Asia. At the same time there were Governors and High Commissioners for Malaya. They were Sir Edward Gent (appointed 29 January 1946), Sir Henry Gurney (appointed 1 October 1948), General Sir Gerald Templer (appointed 15 January 1952) and Sir Donald McGillivray (1 June 1954 to 31 August 1957)

26. President from 23 March 1956.

27. Malaysian Heads of State are elected from among the Rulers for a period of five years.

28. Mr Gopallawa became President of Sri Lanka on 22 May 1972.

29. The Government formed on 1 September 1946 was for an undivided India. This incumbent continued to hold the same post after partition.

30. Aung San was officially Deputy Chairman of the Executive Council of which the Governor was Chairman.

31. Thakin Nu was known as U Nu after March 1952.

32. A Government of Bangladesh in exile was formed on 11 April 1971. All its members, with the exception of the Foreign Minister, K. M. Ahmed, continued to hold office when it moved to Dacca in December 1971.

33. Ministers were abolished with the declaration of Martial Law. The President assumed control of Foreign Affairs and Defence.

34. All Ministries were abolished with the declaration of Martial Law.

35. From 1959 until 1970 Singapore had a Minister of the Interior who was also Minister of Defence. The names listed are those of the Minister of Home Affairs.

36. A member of the Government of all-India who did not continue in the same office after partition.

37. Stevenson was appointed Governor on 1 May 1925. Before that he and his predecessors had been High Commissioners.

38. The post of Prime Minister was abolished when its incumbent became Head of State.

39. After the outbreak of communal violence in Cyprus Turkish Ministers ceased to exercise their functions although they were nominally still in charge of their Departments. Georghadjis acted as Minister of Defence from 1 July 1964.

40. Denton was the first Governor of Gambia. His predecessors were styled Administrator.

41. Bell was the first Governor of Uganda. His predecessors were styled Commissioner.

42. The colony of Nigeria came into existence on 1 January 1914, created from the two Protectorates of Northern and Southern Nigeria. The High Commissioners of Northern Nigeria from 1900 were Sir Frederick Lugard (until September 1906), Sir Percy Girouard (from 1907), Sir Hesketh Bell (from 30 December 1909) and Sir Frederick Lugard again from September 1912. The High Commissioners for Southern Nigeria from 1900 were Sir Ralph Moor (until 1903), Sir Walter Egerton (from 3 Apr 1904) and Sir Frederick Lugard from September 1912.

43. Macpherson was Governor-General from 1 October 1954.

44. Arden-Clarke was Governor-General from 6 March 1957.

45. Turnbull was Governor-General from 9 December 1961.

46. Became President on this date.

47. Dr Azikiwe, appointed as Governor General, became President on 1 October 1963.

48. Coutts became Governor-General on 9 October 1962.

49. Paul became Governor-General on 17 February 1965.

50. Nyerere became President of Tanganyika on that date. On 27 April 1964 he became President of the United Republic of Tanganyika and Zanzibar, and the name of this State was changed to Tanzania on 29 October 1964. The Sultans of Zanzibar in this century have been Hamoud bin Mohammed, Ali bin Hamoud (succeeded 18 August 1902), Sir Khalifa bin Harub (succeeded 15 November 1911), Sir Abdullah bin Khalifa (succeeded 17 October 1960) and Jamshid bin Abdullah (succeeded 1 July 1963). A Revolution broke out on 12 January 1964 when Sheikh Obeid Karume became President. After the union with Tanganyika, although nominally First Vice President of Tanzania, he continued to exercise effective power in Zanzibar until his murder in April 1972. Aboud Jumbe was appointed to succeed him on 12 April 1972. The Prime Ministers of Zanzibar have been Sheikh Muhammad Shamte Hamadi (appointed 5 June 1961) and Sheikh Abdullah Kassim Hanga (appointed 12 January 1964).

51. MacDonald became Governor-General on 12 October 1963.

52. General Ironsi's title was President of the Supreme Military Council.

53. General Ankrah's title was Chairman of the National Liberation Council.

54. General Gowon's title was Chairman of the Federal Military Government.

55. Colonel Juxon-Smith's title was Chairman of the National Reformation Council.

56. Colonel Acheampong's title was Chairman of the National Redemption Council.

57. From July 1954 until the military coup of 19 January 1966 there were Premiers for the three Regions of Nigeria. These were:

   (a) *Eastern Region*
July	1954	De Nnamdi Azikiwe
Jan	1960	Dr Michael Okpara

   (b) *Northern Region*
July	1954	Alhaji Sir Ahmadu Bello, Sardauna of Sokoto

   (c) *Western Region*
July	1954	Chief Awolowo
Dec	1959	Samuel Ladoke Akintola
May	1962	Alhaji Dawodu Adegbenro
May	1962	Post abolished—state of emergency
Jan	1963	Samuel Ladoke Akintola

   In January 1966 Military Governors were appointed.

58. In April 1962 Jomo Kenyatta and Ronald Ngalo became in effect joint Heads of Government. This arrangement lasted until June 1963 when Kenyatta became sole Prime Minister.

59. The post was abolished after a military coup.

60. Odaka was appointed Minister of State on this date to deal with Foreign Affairs and was later formally appointed Minister of Foreign Affairs.

61. President Kenyatta remained Minister of Foreign Affairs until 1969 but the Ministers listed did much of the routine work and were often referred to as Ministers of Foreign Affairs.

62. Although Sir Dauda Jawara remained formally Minister of Foreign Affairs until 1967, much of the routine work was done by Alhaji A. B. Njie, who was often referred to as Minister of Foreign Affairs.

63. Sokoine was the first head of a separately consituted Ministry of Defence. President

Nyerere, Rashidi Kawawa and Oscar Kambona were at times in charge of Defence in addition to holding other posts.

64. Gambians listed are Ministers of Local Government.

65. The date given is that on which Lesotho became an independent State. Moeshoeshoe II had been Chief of the Basuto people since he came of age in February 1960.

66. The date given is that on which Swaziland became an independent State. Sobhuza II had been Chief of the Swazi people since 1921.

67. Sir Seretse Khama has been Minister of Foreign Affairs since September 1966. He has been assisted by the following Ministers of State: Moutlakgola Nwako (appointed September 1966), E. Setlhomo Masisi (appointed October 1969) and Bakwena Kgari (appointed April 1972). These have sometimes been referred to as Ministers of Foreign Affairs.

68. In Malawi the Ministry of Home Affairs was abolished and separate Ministers for the Regions appointed. With a Minister a Local Government.

69. Blackburne became Governor-General on 6 August 1962.

70. Hochoy became Governor-General on 31 August 1962.

71. On the formation of the Federation of the West Indies in April 1958, Sir Grantley Adams became Federal Prime Minister. Foreign Affairs and Defence were left in the hands of officials, there was no Minister of the Interior. The Minster of Finance was Robert Bradshaw, subsequently Premier of St Kitts. These two remained in office until the dissolution of the Federation in 1962. The Governor-General was Lord Hailes.

72. Although Burnham remained Foreign Minister until 1972, he was assisted firstly by Deeoroop Mahraj and then by S. S. Ramphal. These were sometimes referred to as Ministers of Foreign Affairs.

73. Western Samoa had joint Heads of State until the death of Tupua Tamasa Mea'ole on 5 April 1963. After that date Malietoa Tanumafili II was sole Head of State.

74. The Ministers in this column were the Chief Ministers of Travancore until 1 July 1949. On that date a reorganisation led to the state of Travancore-Cochin. A further reorganisation in 1956 led to the creation of the state of Kerala.

75. The State of Maharasthra came into existence after the division of the State of Bombay into Maharasthra and Gujerat. Chavan who had been chief Minister of Bombay became Chief Minister of Maharasthra.

76. The name of Madras State was changed to Tamil Nadu in 1968.